POWER PLAY
The Business Economics of Pro Sports

Glen Hodgson and Mario Lefebvre

The Conference Board of Canada Ottawa, Ontario March 2014

©2014 The Conference Board of Canada*
All rights reserved.
ISBN: 978-1-928073-00-0
Agreement No. 40063028
*Incorporated as AERIC Inc.

The Conference Board of Canada
255 Smyth Road, Ottawa ON K1H 8M7 Canada
Inquiries 1-866-711-2262
conferenceboard.ca

Library and Archives Canada Cataloguing in Publication

Hodgson, Glen David, 1955-, author
      Power play : the business economics of pro sports / Glen Hodgson,
Mario Lefebvre.

Includes bibliographical references.
Issued in print and electronic formats.
ISBN 978-1-928073-00-0 (pbk.).--ISBN 978-1-928073-01-7 (epub)

      1. Professional sports--Economic aspects--Canada. I. Lefebvre,
Mario, 1967-, author II. Conference Board of Canada III. Title.

GV716.H63 2014   338.4'77960971   C2014-901209-8
                                                C2014-901210-1

Printed and bound in Canada by Gilmore Printing.

Table of Contents

Preface

Dave Naylor

It was the spring of 2010 and I was working on a TSN series, titled "Why Not Canada?" about potential additional Canadian NHL markets. It was a complicated assignment on a subject that had no shortage of conjecture or opinion. What it lacked was a lot of facts— actual economic data or a study that could speak to the readiness of places such as Winnipeg, Hamilton, or Québec City to welcome NHL franchises.

While driving from Montréal to Québec City, where we were to interview the city's mayor, Régis Labeaume, I began racking my brain for ways to fill the void of information about local economies in Canada.

During that drive, I thought of Brent Dowdall, the media relations head at The Conference Board of Canada, with whom I had crossed paths through mutual friends at Carleton University. We didn't speak often, but something told me he might be able to help.

So while my cameraman took the wheel, I pulled out my phone, reached Brent and explained my dilemma to him.

"Have I got the right guy for you … " he said.

But Mario Lefebvre wasn't in the office that day. He was, by sheer coincidence, in Québec City for a few days.

Call it fate that the very next day I got to meet and interview a man whose research and knowledge would become central to my six-part series.

I like to think that I helped scratch the surface of Mario's curiosity about the relationship between Canadian economics and professional sports teams. What I did not know then was that Mario had a "twin in kind" at The Conference Board of Canada in Glen Hodgson. Over the next few years, as Glen and Mario's ongoing research projects were released for public consumption, I realized they were establishing a comprehensive area of expertise where once so little had existed. It was as if they'd set out to measure every factor there was in why a team may or may not make it.

The result is what you hold in your hands today.

So while I may have helped pass the puck out of the zone on this area of study, it is Glen and Mario's hard work, expertise, and dedication that's allowed them to bury it in the top corner with this book.

Dave Naylor, November 2013

Introduction

Why This Book?

Why would two economists write a book on the business economics of pro sports? The simple answer is that we both have had a passion for sports since childhood, both as competitive athletes and as fans. Each of us was good enough to play amateur sports at a high competitive level up to the junior age group, but (unfortunately) neither of us was quite good enough to advance to the top competitive levels.

So, like most other wishful athletes, we found other ways to develop our talents. We studied economics as young adults and have had reasonably successful careers doing economic analysis and providing policy advice to governments and businesses. Yet, all the while, our passion for sports continued to burn bright. We "stayed in the game" by competing against other adults in various sports, coaching youth sports, and following the top-level pro sports leagues and athletes. With this book, we finally found a way to combine our lifelong interest in sports with our analytical abilities as professional economists.

The book started innocently enough in 2010 with a few ideas that we kicked around on why some professional sports franchises and leagues succeed while others are disasters. The back-and-forth discussion between us eventually turned into a first commentary—defining the pro sports market in Canada—which was posted on The Conference Board of Canada's website. The media took an interest, which prompted us to keep discussing and defining various economic and business aspects of pro sports and writing other commentaries. Gradually an analytical structure began to take shape (hey ... we are economists after all) and we completed the structure to create what we believe is a complete economic analysis of pro sports from a Canadian perspective. We hope you agree!

We would like to thank the many external reviewers and colleagues who took the time to read and critique one or more of the commentaries that form the foundation of this book. The list of external reviewers includes Jim Kyte, Dave Best, Jeffrey Simpson, Roy MacGregor, Brian Ward, Ian Lee, Christopher Ragan, Tim Ragan, and Christopher Waddell. Conference Board colleagues who reviewed material include Craig MacLaine (master editor and super Habs fan), Brent Dowdall, Todd Crawford, Derek Hughes, Michael Grant, Steve Lugtigheid, and Perry Eisenschmid. We extend thanks as well to Alan Arcand, who helped dig out the data, and to the members of the Publishing team at the Conference Board, which transformed this material into a polished final product ready for publication.

Finally, we want to thanks our wives—Christina Caron and Peggy Bachman—for their love and support, their understanding of the many hours we spent hunched in front of a computer screen writing this book, and their patience at being dragged to many hockey, baseball, and football games and other sporting events. We know you probably would have preferred to be doing something else, but you truly were "good sports"!

We hope you, the reader, enjoy this book and that you learn a bit more about the business economics of pro sports.

Glen Hodgson and Mario Lefebvre

Chapter 1
The Pro Sports Market in Canada

Fans live and breathe sports. Their emotions soar and plunge alongside the fortunes of their favourite teams. But pro sports are more than just a passion—they are, first and foremost, big business.

Professional sports teams hold a special place in the hearts of many of us. Sports fans everywhere—including millions of Canadians—feel a deep emotional attachment to "their team." The team brand matters. There is a strong sense of loyalty to that brand, and there is the emotional roller-coaster that many of us ride with every win or loss.

Witness the behaviour of Montréalers in the spring of 2010 as the Canadiens progressed through to the third round of the Stanley Cup playoffs—much further than almost anyone had expected. Fans poured out into the streets after each game to wildly celebrate a Canadiens victory or to mourn a loss. Similar scenes have played out along Calgary's Red Mile, and in downtown Edmonton and Ottawa when those cities' NHL teams made it to the Cup final in recent years.

The ultimate Canadian team—the one that brings together fans of all ages from across the country—is the men's Team Canada hockey squad, assembled every four years for the Winter Olympic Games. When Sidney Crosby scored the "golden goal" to defeat the U.S. in overtime and give Canada the gold medal at the 2010 Winter Games in Vancouver, the country cheered as one. And we cheered again in 2014 when the Canadian men and women pulled off a second straight pair of gold medals—a "golden double-double"—in hockey at Sochi.

Conversely, witness the agony felt by Canadian fans as they watched the country's best juniors collapse in the third period and lose to Russia in the gold-medal game of the 2011 World Junior Hockey Championships. Such pain is not limited to hockey. Saskatchewan fans thought their Roughriders had won the 2009 Grey Cup. But their joy was put on hold when a penalty for too many men on the field gave the rival Montreal Alouettes one more chance to kick a field goal for the victory and the Cup. The kick was good. The Als were suddenly the victors rather than the vanquished. And the Roughrider fans were crushed.

Perhaps the longest-lasting pain has been felt by hockey fans in Québec City and baseball fans in Montréal, who lost their teams when the Nordiques moved to Colorado in 1995 and the Expos left for Washington in 2004. Hockey fans in Winnipeg also suffered the pain of losing their team when their Jets moved to Phoenix in 1996. (They, however, have since recovered, thanks to the surprising announcement in the spring of 2011 that the NHL's Atlanta franchise was moving to Winnipeg and being rebranded as the Jets.) Then, of course, there is the never-ending pain suffered by Leafs fans, for whom it has been 46 years, and counting, since their team last won the Stanley Cup. The long gone but not forgotten (nor lamented) former Leafs owner, Harold Ballard, haunts them still.

> Perhaps the longest-lasting pain has been felt by hockey fans in Québec City and baseball fans in Montréal, who lost their teams when the Nordiques moved to Colorado in 1995 and the Expos left for Washington in 2004.

The events in Québec City, Montréal, and Winnipeg remind us that there is an important dimension to pro sports teams. They are not just sources of pride or misery (civic or personal)—they are also businesses. (That pro sports teams are referred to as "franchises" within a defined league underlines this fact.) The emotion of fan support can sustain a team in the short term. But, with few exceptions, economic forces rule over the longer term and a franchise must be financially viable. Some pro teams remain "cash cows" whether they win or lose. A few are the personal possessions of very wealthy owners who aren't that concerned if the team makes money or not. Others become money pits for owners who do care about making money, and these teams eventually move, are sold, or simply fold. There is also another economic layer attached to sports franchises— the socio-economic impact of a franchise on the surrounding community.

What, then, are the conditions that make a professional sports team successful—at the bank, and maybe even on the field or rink? And what are the various economic impacts of professional team sports? That is the subject of this book, as written by two self-confessed jock economists. Our analysis begins with a look at Canada's pro sports market.

The Pro Sports Market in Canada

There are many professional sports leagues and teams operating in Canada. And while hockey is the most popular professional team sport in Canada, professional football, baseball, and basketball all have a wide Canadian audience. The popularity of pro football is rising quickly and steadily, thanks to superb marketing by the National Football League (NFL) and the ongoing success—particularly out West—of the Canadian Football League (CFL). After at least two false starts, professional soccer in Canada is also on a growth path, with three teams now in the ranks of North America's premier soccer league— Major League Soccer (MLS). Toronto FC was first to join, followed by Vancouver in 2011 and Montréal in 2012. Pro indoor lacrosse (or "box" lacrosse) also has its moments of mainstream success, with National Lacrosse League teams in four Canadian cities.

Most of these team sports also have professional leagues at the minor-league level. These minor leagues act as professional training grounds for pro athletes trying to make it to the top. There are four

American Hockey League (AHL) franchises operating in Canada. It can be argued that top-tier junior hockey is also a professional minor league—although the players receive modest stipends rather than salaries. This level of quasi-professional hockey is played under the banner of the Canadian Hockey League and is spread across three top-tier junior leagues that operate in Québec and Atlantic Canada (the QMJHL), Ontario (the OHL), and Western Canada (the WHL). These leagues have franchises in cities and town across Canada,.as well as in several U.S. communities.

Minor league baseball in Canada dates back to 1854 with the founding of the Young Canadians of Hamilton. Teams have existed in many Canadian cities and in many different leagues ever since.[1] There has been a high degree of turnover in Canadian minor league baseball franchises in recent years, and teams are more and more likely today to be independent operations without a major league affiliate. There have also been minor league professional basketball teams operating in Canada from time to time (including the National Basketball League of Canada, which started up in 2011), and there have been professional soccer teams competing outside the MLS.

Whatever the league or the level, Canadians have long had a rich mix of professional team sports events from which to choose.

Keeping track of pro sports franchises is always a challenge since they are in a seemingly continuous state of change. Table 1 provides a snapshot of franchises across the country, as of September 2013.

As of September 2013, Canada was home to seven NHL franchises, eight CFL franchises, one MLB franchise, one NBA franchise, three MLS franchises, and four NLL franchises. There are also American Hockey League (AHL) franchises in Abbotsford, Hamilton, Toronto, and St. John's. Though not considered "major" league, the AHL is a true professional league.

---

1   One of the briefing's authors has an uncle who played baseball in the Northern League back in the 1950s for the Winnipeg Goldeyes—surely one of the best team names ever!

Table 1
Major League Canadian Professional Sports Franchises by City and League

	National Hockey League	Canadian Football League	Major League Baseball	National Basketball Association	Major League Soccer	National Lacrosse League
Calgary	Flames	Stampeders				Roughnecks
Edmonton	Oilers	Eskimos				Rush
Hamilton		Tiger-Cats				
Montréal	Canadiens	Alouettes	Expos (1969–2004)		Impact	
Ottawa–Gatineau	Senators	Rough Riders (1876–1996) Renegades (2001–06) Redblacks (2014–)				
Québec City	Nordiques (1979–95)					
Regina		Saskatchewan Roughriders				
Toronto	Maple Leafs	Argonauts	Blue Jays	Raptors	Toronto FC	Rock
Vancouver	Canucks	BC Lions		Grizzlies (1995–2001)	Whitecaps	Stealth
Winnipeg	Jets (1979–96), (2011–)	Blue Bombers				

Source: The Conference Board of Canada.

How Big Is the Canadian Pro Sports Market?

One of The Conference Board of Canada's key areas of expertise is estimating and evaluating the economic footprint of various sectors of the Canadian economy. In a perfect world, we would measure and evaluate, in detail, the economic footprint of Canada's professional team sports market or sector, using Statistics Canada aggregate data as a foundation, and providing our own estimates of the economic effects. A detailed assessment would need to take into account a wide variety of factors, including the direct and indirect benefits for the economy of these franchises, and the "leakages" from our economy in terms of imports, savings, and player salaries that are eventually transferred abroad. However, producing that kind of detailed estimate of the economic footprint of a specific sector requires significant staff time. To complete this task, the Conference Board would require the financial support of a project sponsor.

Nevertheless, acquiring the data for assessing the estimated revenues and operating income of most professional sports teams— key pieces of information in any detailed estimation of the economic footprint of the professional team sport market or sector in Canada—is relatively easy.

Let's start with Canada's National Hockey League franchises. These franchises are privately owned businesses, and their detailed financial reports are not released directly. However, because professional sports leagues usually have a revenue-sharing agreement and/or a collective agreement with their players, they have to file their financial results with the league office. This information then enters the public forum through team valuations that are done every year, with estimates provided by the U.S.-based, business media giant Forbes being the most widely used. Such is the case for the NHL.

The Forbes estimates of revenues and profitability for Canadian teams in the NHL, MLB, and NBA are provided in Table 2. With the Canadian dollar trading at a relatively minor discount to the U.S. dollar, the exchange rate essentially can be taken out of the current estimates.

Table 2

Estimated Canadian NHL, MLB, and NBA Franchise Revenues and Operating Income, 2012

($ millions)

Franchise	Revenues	Operating income
Toronto Maple Leafs	200	81.9
Montreal Canadiens	169	51.6
Vancouver Canucks	143	30.4
Calgary Flames	117	11.0
Edmonton Oilers	106	16.2
Ottawa Senators	113	14.5
Winnipeg Jets	105	13.3
Toronto Raptors	121	18.8
Toronto Blue Jays	203	−4.8

Note: NHL team valuations as of November 2012, with numbers from the 2011–12 season; Raptors' valuation as of January 2013, using the 2011–12 season revenues; Blue Jays' valuation as of March 2013, using the 2012 revenues.
Source: Forbes.

(Canadian NHL teams pay their players in U.S. dollars, while most of their revenues are in Canadian dollars—so the exchange rate matters to their financial results.)

This information can be corroborated through the team salary cap as negotiated by the NHL and its players. For the 2011–12 season (prior to the recent lockout and the new salary cap system), the overall cap was equal to 57 per cent of the teams' operating revenues, or US$64.3 million per team. We therefore know that NHL teams generated, on average, revenues of about US$113 million in 2011–12. Anecdotal evidence, as shown in Table 3, indicates that five of the seven Canadian NHL teams are near or well above the league average in home attendance, so we know the league average would be a conservative revenue floor for each Canadian team.

In short, the available data suggest that, although there are sharp differences among the teams in terms of operating income, the seven Canadian NHL franchises have a revenue footprint within the Canadian economy of about $800 million.

Table 3
Canadian NHL Teams—Average Attendance
(per game, after 20 home games, 2012–13 season)

Rank	Franchise	Attendance
2	Montreal Canadiens	21,273
5	Toronto Maple Leafs	19,426
6	Ottawa Senators	19,408
7	Calgary Flames	19,289
10	Vancouver Canucks	18,947
24	Edmonton Oilers	16,839
27	Winnipeg Jets	15,004

Sources: ESPN; National Hockey League.

The window into the CFL's finances is also quite transparent. Three CFL teams are "community-owned." These teams have a very large number of small investors and a business model, balance sheet, and income statement that have been built up step-by-step over a long period of time. And because they are community-owned, the financial reports for these CFL franchises are widely available to the public. In 2012, the Saskatchewan Roughriders had yet another profitable year, although profits were somewhat lower than in recent years. The team reported a profit of $1.1 million in 2012 on gross revenues of $34.4 million. The lower profit was attributable to the large increase in amortization expenses associated with the Grey Cup Legacy Project at Mosaic Stadium. As Grey Cup host in 2013, the Riders no doubt generated strong revenues and profits. The Edmonton Eskimos reported $8.8 million in operating revenue for the 2012 business year, and net operating income of just over $207,060. Lastly, the Winnipeg Blue Bombers reported operating revenue for the 2012 business year of $16.7 million, with a loss of $758,307. However, the loss was entirely attributed to increased stadium development costs and a loss on disposal of stadium assets. In comparison, the Blue Bombers recorded a profit of over $2.3 million in 2011.

This public financial reporting from three long-time and stable CFL franchises suggests that the CFL generates annual revenues between $120 million and $150 million (again, with a significant variation in revenues and earnings among the teams).

The Toronto Blue Jays and Raptors also generate significant annual operating revenues. The Forbes data in Table 2 indicate that these two franchises generate over $320 million in annual revenue. Generally, both teams have operated profitably. But the Blue Jays did show a loss in 2012, and the significant rise in their 2013 payroll (a result of adding several stars to their rosters via free agency) is raising a question mark about their 2013 overall financial performance. Hopes were high for this team going into the 2013 season, but the Blue Jays finished last in the very competitive American League East Division. Nonetheless, the team still managed to attract 2.5 million fans to its home games in 2013, which should prop up the overall revenue numbers. Lastly, the three MLS franchises listed in Table 1 will obviously generate additional pro sports revenues going forward, as will the NLL and the various minor league teams.

Hosting the World Junior Hockey Championships has become an almost annual event in Canada. Canada hosted the tournament in 2006, 2009, 2010, and 2012. And Canada is already scheduled to host it every second year starting in 2015 through to 2021. According to the Canadian Sports Tourism Alliance, the 2012 tournament in Calgary generated an estimated $86 million in total economic activity and a profit of $22 million, which was to be distributed by Hockey Canada to hockey programs and facilities across the country. So junior hockey can be big business, too.

Hosting the World Junior Hockey Championships has become an almost annual event in Canada.

Even curling—with its Brier championship and pro circuit—could be added to the list of team sports that generate significant revenue and local economic benefits.

Non-team pro sports—such as golf, tennis, motor sports, boxing, and mixed martial arts—also generate significant revenue in Canada.

The most lucrative once-a-year professional sport event in Canada is the annual Formula One (F1) event in Montréal. On average, 110,000 people attend the Fl race itself, and 300,000 attend at least one F1 event over the race weekend (two days of qualifying, followed by the race on Sunday). A typical ticket package for the full event is about $300, which includes a $200 seat (approx.) for the official race on Sunday. Tickets for the best seats are considerably higher than that. Overall, our back-of-the-envelope estimate is that ticket sales alone for the F1 event could be as high as $40 million.

Given the significant economic multiplier benefits for a community holding the race—including spending on accommodation, travel, meals and drink, and related entertainment, as well as the F1 event itself—it's no surprise that governments at the local, provincial, and federal levels all fought hard to convince the F1 organizers to return to Montréal after a one-year absence in 2009.

In sum, our simple estimations indicate that combined pro sports revenues for Canada are at least $1.5 billion annually, but likely even higher. (A deeper economic analysis would include the additional economic multiplier effects—but also the leakages—for communities, regions, and for the economy as a whole.) Overall, professional sports are more than just entertainment in Canada—they are big business.

Chapter 2
Defining the Market Conditions for Success

Fan passion is critical to the success of a pro sports franchise. The fans faithfully buy the tickets and the merchandise, and watch the television coverage that brings in the ad revenues. But on its own, passion is not enough. In the pro sports business, success or failure also rides on the existence—or lack—of some key market conditions.

Every local or regional market has fundamental characteristics that can be assessed to determine whether a pro sports franchise can succeed in that particular market. When assessing such a market, we want to know whether it has what we call the "market conditions for success."

Of course, the local population's love or passion for the game has to be a part of the equation. That's a given. No matter how populous or fortunate a region is, if fan passion for the game does not exist, the team will fail.

Our assumption is that individuals and/or corporations that try to bring professional teams to their communities have already satisfied themselves that there is a love for the game there. (We will look at the issue of fan passion—and what happens when the passion is gone—in later chapters.)

Aside from passion, therefore, the success of a professional sports organization in any given market relies on four pillars of support. They are:

- market size;
- income levels;
- a strong corporate presence;
- a level playing field.

Pillar One: Market Size

Every professional team requires strong fan support to be financially sustainable. Empty seats in the stands mean fewer tickets sold and lower revenues from souvenir and concession stand sales and parking. In addition to fan support, a successful pro sports franchise will generally need strong corporate or business support and healthy broadcasting revenues in order to survive.

What size population base is needed for a city or region to support a professional team? We believe that the following rule of thumb is reasonable: The population of a market must be at least equal to the potential total number of tickets sold in a season.

No matter how populous or fortunate a region is, if fan passion for the game does not exist, the team will fail.

According to this hypothesis, the minimum market size needed to support a Canadian Football League team is about 250,000 (one pre-season game plus nine regular season home games, multiplied by 25,000 fans per game). A National Hockey League team in Canada needs a little over 800,000 potential fans (4 pre-season games plus 41 regular season games, multiplied by 18,000 fans per game), and a Major League Baseball team needs a home market population of almost 2,500,000 (81 home games times 30,000 fans per game). Thus, based on this first pillar, Regina can support a CFL team, but it doesn't come close to being able to support an NHL team.

Population in the Market Must Be Rising

Another element—sound population growth—must be added to this first pillar. It is one thing to have the fan base required right now, but it is just as important that the fan base be there in the future. A market not only needs a large enough population today, it also needs a population that is growing. The need for growth stems mainly from the phenomenon of aging. The population in Canada is aging at a rapid pace, and we can assume that as citizens age they become less likely to attend professional sports events, due to income restraints and fading interest. It is therefore imperative for the success of a pro sports franchise that the community posts solid population growth, thereby ensuring that it will possess the required fan base for years to come.

Let's use a few numbers to illustrate this need for a growing population. Our rule of thumb for pillar one suggests that the fan base required to support an NHL team is about 800,000. On average, people aged 65 and over made up about 15 per cent of Canada's population in 2010. So, on average, a community of 800,000 last year had a total of 680,000 people aged 64 or younger. With no growth in the population, and based on current demographic trends in Canada, by 2025 that same community of 800,000 would have 600,000 citizens aged 64 or younger. That's a drop of about 12 per cent over 15 years in the population aged 64 or younger—a drop that would be detrimental to, for example, the health of a local NHL franchise. To maintain a population of 680,000 aged 64 or younger, the overall head count would need to increase to 910,000, a rise of 0.9 per cent per year (and a rate that is very much in line with the pace at which Canada's population is rising).

The rapid rise in immigration is another reason why growth in the population is required. While this is hard to quantify, foreign-born Canadians are less likely to have grown up with hockey, football, or baseball, and are therefore less likely to be as passionate about these sports as Canadian-born citizens. The steady rise in the ratio of foreign-born to total population in Canada's urban areas is yet another reason why population growth is required in order to provide a sufficiently large and ongoing fan base.

> There is a limit to how far any one market can be stretched by adding additional pro sports teams to the mix. Market saturation will occur at some point.

A word of caution—there is a limit to the number of different sports franchises any market can absorb. Since there are sports fans who have both the interest and the income to support teams in multiple sports, the fan base required for an additional franchise is additive; that is, the required fan base per franchise is not mutually exclusive. Nonetheless, there is a limit to how far any one market can be stretched by adding additional pro sports teams to the mix. Market saturation will occur at some point. (We will explore this issue in greater depth in future chapters.)

Pillar Two: Income Levels

For a market to be able to support a professional sports team today, it must have a relatively high-income population. Attending a professional sports event can be expensive. Is there a minimum per capita income needed to support a professional sports franchise? Again, there are no formal rules, and the Conference Board has not conducted specific data-driven research.

However, to see whether there is an observed relationship between income level and possible franchise success, let's compare the level of disposable income per capita in cities that do have National Hockey League franchises with that of cities that have the right market size (our first pillar) but do not have NHL franchises.

As shown in Table 4, the level of disposable income per capita in the two metropolitan areas that have sufficient populations but do not have NHL teams (Hamilton and Québec City) are not the lowest among the nine metropolitan areas listed. In fact, Montréal—home to one of the NHL's most successful franchises—has the lowest level of disposable income per capita. But with a population and fan base of nearly 4,000,000, Greater Montréal's absolute size more than compensates for its slightly lower average disposable income. (It is also worth noting that Québec City's per capita income ranking has improved since it lost its NHL franchise in the mid-1990s.)

Table 4
Disposable Income Per Capita in Canada's Large Metropolitan Areas
($, rank)

Census metropolitan area	Disposable income per capita, 1995 (rank)	Disposable income per capita, 2012 (rank)
Calgary	21,279 (1)	42,877 (1)
Edmonton	17,950 (7)	37,920 (2)
Ottawa–Gatineau	20,023 (3)	34,344 (3)
Toronto	20,112 (2)	30,473 (4)
Vancouver	19,384 (5)	30,020 (5)
Hamilton	19,639 (4)	29,633 (6)
Québec City	17,584 (8)	28,903 (7)
Winnipeg	18,192 (6)	28,564 (8)
Montréal	16,751 (9)	26,722 (9)

Sources: The Conference Board of Canada; Statistics Canada.

Other Canadian census metropolitan areas (CMAs)—Regina, Saskatoon, and Kitchener–Waterloo–Cambridge (KWC), for example—have levels of personal disposable income that are very much comparable to those that appear in Table 4. While these three CMAs do not have sufficient market size (our first pillar) to support an NHL franchise, Saskatoon and KWC may have large enough populations to support a Canadian Football League (CFL) franchise. (Chapter 11 is devoted entirely to the CFL and the potential for other CFL franchises in Canada.)

Pillar Three: A Strong Corporate Presence

The third pillar required to support a pro sports franchise is the presence in the region of corporate head offices. Filling your arena or stadium every night is good, but filling dozens of corporate boxes every night is even better. The rental rate for corporate boxes is high relative to the rates for other seats in the stadium. The same holds true for the price of food and drinks served in the boxes. Plus, boxes can generate sponsorship and other revenues. And even if a stadium does not have corporate boxes, the relatively higher income of employees in head offices will help to support the fan base.

Table 5 provides the number of corporate head offices per metropolitan area for selected Canadian cities.

Table 5
Corporate Presence in Canada's Largest Urban Centres, 2012
(corporate head offices, per cent)

Census metropolitan area	Number of corporate headquarters (percentage share)
1. Toronto	253 (31.6%)
2. Calgary	135 (16.9%)
3. Montréal	97 (12.1%)
4. Vancouver	94 (11.8%)
5. Winnipeg	26 (3.3%)
6. Edmonton	22 (2.8%)
7. Ottawa–Gatineau	18 (2.3%)
8. Québec City	14 (1.8%)
9. Kitchener–Cambridge–Waterloo	12 (1.5%)
10. Saskatoon	11 (1.4%)
11. Hamilton	8 (1.0%)
12. Halifax	8 (1.0%)
13. Regina	8 (1.0%)

Sources: *Financial Post*, 2012 list of Canada's 800 largest companies by revenue.

Undeniably, Toronto, Calgary, Montréal, and Vancouver are in a league of their own on this criterion. In fact, Toronto is well ahead of everyone else; the head offices of 253 of Canada's 800 largest corporations—31.6 per cent—are located in the Toronto metropolitan area. Calgary (135), Montréal (97), and Vancouver (94) are relatively close to each other in terms of head office numbers. After that, the numbers drop off sharply. Fifth-place Winnipeg is home to 22 of Canada's 800 largest corporations, trailing far behind fourth-place Vancouver. Winnipeg finds itself slightly ahead of Edmonton (22) and Ottawa–Gatineau (18). Québec City is in eighth place, at 14, not far behind Ottawa–Gatineau.[1] Given the relatively low presence of large corporations in Québec City, which is trying to bring back an NHL franchise, a smart move would be to secure corporate engagement beforehand. This is exactly what the city is trying to do, lining up a relatively firm list of would-be corporate sponsors behind its bid to bring an NHL franchise back to replace the Nordiques (who moved to Colorado in 1995).

Pillar Four: A Level Playing Field

If a metropolitan area has the fan base, both in size and in relative income, and the necessary corporate presence, does that guarantee success? Not quite. Our fourth macroeconomic pillar for success is a level playing field. Two items in particular are part of this pillar: the exchange rate and the tax burden. In the case of a league—such as the CFL—that has all of its operations in one country, the exchange rate does not play a significant role. Nearly all of the CFL's revenues are denominated in Canadian dollars, as are its costs. Neither does the tax burden play a significant role. True, the overall tax burden for businesses and individuals is heavier in Québec than it is in Alberta. But we have yet to hear a CFL player say he'd rather play in Calgary

---

1   The large presence of the federal government in Ottawa also puts that city at a disadvantage relative to other cities in Canada because of the federal "hospitality" rules. Senior civil servants, unlike executives in the private sector, are barred from accepting free tickets to games from suppliers. This can make it more difficult to sell corporate boxes in the Ottawa market, as these seats are often used by the box owners as a way to promote their businesses or to show clients their appreciation.

or Edmonton than in Montréal because he will pay less tax playing for a team located in Alberta. (Maybe the nightlife in Montréal provides a balancing influence.)

If a metropolitan area has the fan base, both in size and in relative income, and the necessary corporate presence, does that guarantee success? Not quite.

However, when the league operates in more than one country—as is the case for the National Hockey League, Major League Baseball, Major League Soccer, and even pro lacrosse—the exchange rate and the tax burden can become significant barriers to the success of a franchise. Imagine when both of these factors are working against a market, as was the case in the mid-1990s for the original Winnipeg Jets (who moved to Phoenix in 1996) and the Quebec Nordiques. Back then, Québec City and Winnipeg residents faced much higher marginal income tax rates than did their U.S. counterparts. That was a major strike against these teams at the time, and it remains a concern for Canadian teams to this day. And, of course, while fans with higher incomes are more likely to buy tickets, they are also burdened with the highest marginal tax rates—which diminishes their capacity to buy tickets.

On top of this heavier tax burden, Canadian franchises in the mid-1990s were being squeezed by the weakness of the Canadian dollar. At the time, the Canadian currency was worth about US$0.75. (And it would continue to lose ground, dropping below US$0.62 in January 2002!) This negative exchange rate effect was devastating for Canadian NHL teams, since they are required to pay their players in U.S. dollars. The same was true for baseball's Toronto Blue Jays and Montreal Expos. For example, a player who was paid a salary of US$2.5 million in the mid-1990s would cost his Canadian team almost C$3.5 million. On a payroll of US$25 million, this negative exchange rate effect would add almost C$10 million to the cost base of Canadian teams compared with their U.S.-based rivals. This painful exchange rate situation led to a sharp rise in revenue requirements to cover player salaries and became a serious financial issue for numerous

Canadian NHL franchises and both of Canada's Major League Baseball teams. It may not have been the only factor that compelled the Jets and Nordiques to leave for greener pastures (as the Expos would also do in 2004), but it certainly was a major contributing factor.

What About the Economic Outlook?

Should the economic outlook for a given market be considered a pillar for success? We are reluctant to say so, since economic fluctuations occur everywhere. Even Calgary, a city some thought immune to economic downturns not so long ago, was hit hard by the 2008–09 recession. There will always be economic fluctuations, and there is little reason to believe that one city will be hit more frequently or harder than any other city. Therefore, while recognizing that the economic outlook is important, we do not include it as a market pillar for success.

Conclusion

Basic economics matter fundamentally to the financial success of a professional sports franchise in a given market. There are four market pillars:

- **Market size**—Having a large enough population is key to ensuring that seats will be filled every night. Moreover, faced with changing demographics and an aging population, communities with a growing population will be better positioned to offer continuing support to their professional sports franchise.
- **Income levels**—Relatively high income levels are required, since attending a professional sports event is expensive.
- **A sound corporate presence**—Sufficient corporate support is a must. Filling the stands with fans is great, but corporate sponsorship and full corporate boxes are critical additional sources of revenue.
- **A level playing field**—Teams have a tough time succeeding if they are not able to compete on a level playing field. The weak exchange rate of the 1990s and early 2000s (which hurt Canadian NHL franchises in particular) and the sharp differences between Canadian and U.S. taxation levels tilted the field against Canadian franchises. A level field is needed.

If these four market-based pillars exist, they provide a strong foundation for a professional sports franchise's financial success over the long run.

There are, and probably always will be, some wealthy owners for whom money is no object and for whom the possibility of losing a few million dollars a year on their sports franchises is no cause for concern. But for the others—and they make up the majority of franchise owners—the market fundamentals matter.

Chapter 3
Competitive Conditions in Pro Sports Leagues

Sports fans eagerly give their hearts to their favourite teams. But pro sports leagues are full of perennial winners—and losers. Sometimes, winning or losing can be determined by underlying competitive conditions that are not always equal. In this chapter, we analyze the concept of a level playing field as it applies to the various leagues.

The competitive conditions that exist within a pro sports league can be crucial to the success of individual franchises and to the long-term health of the league as a whole. When looking at a given league, we want to know whether it pays more than just lip service to creating the conditions for a level playing field—competitively and financially—among its franchises. Specifically:

- Does the league limit the salaries of players, relative to expected revenue?
- Are revenues shared among the franchises? If so, from which sources, and to what degree?
- Do all teams have equal access to existing and new talent?

- Does the league compensate teams when changes in conditions beyond their control (such as changes in the exchange rate) make them less competitive?
- Moreover, is there a relationship between competitive balance and league profitability?

The answers to these questions will help determine whether a given league has found the right mix of business and on-the-field competitive conditions, and whether a level playing field, our fourth pillar in Chapter 2, has truly been established among its franchises.

Salary Cap and Player Salaries

Most professional sports leagues today have some form of salary cap. In an age of player free agency, a salary cap helps to ensure that franchises can be operated profitably. The cap does this by constraining the ability of players and their agents to bid up player salaries beyond a certain level, and by preventing the richer teams from gaining a competitive advantage by using their wealth to lure talent away from the not-so-rich teams. The salary cap limits total player salary expenses (usually to a percentage of revenues) and allows teams that are well-managed and well-positioned in their market to operate profitably.

In terms of simple economics, a salary cap is usually implemented in response to unequal financial and market power across the league's franchises. Economic theory suggests that if all franchises were equal in economic and competitive strength, and all were driven by the desire to maximize profits, then a salary cap would not be necessary. All teams would have a comparable ability to attract and retain talent, and no one would have an incentive to offer a significantly larger contract than anyone else to a specific player. In the real business world of pro sports, however, such equality does not exist—the financial and business circumstances of franchises vary greatly. Salary caps are therefore created to level the playing field among franchises in terms of player costs.

Salary caps in the various sports leagues are a source of recurring tension between owners and players (the National Hockey League's 2012–13 lockout provided yet another example of this) because they constrain the capacity of players and their agents to maximize salaries through open-market negotiations. The periodic negotiations that take place on the salary cap regime in the various pro sports leagues have produced systems best described as complex and convoluted.

The salary cap limits total player salary expenses (usually to a percentage of revenues) and allows teams that are well-managed and well-positioned in their market to operate profitably.

The salary cap system in place in the NHL establishes the level of the cap, as well as a salary floor, applied to all teams. Under the cap system, a team's total player payroll for the season cannot exceed the maximum or drop below the minimum at any point during the season.

New NHL salary cap levels were negotiated during the collective bargaining agreement (CBA) negotiations that took place in 2012 and into January 2013, during which the players were locked out by the owners. Under the agreement that ended the lockout, a cap of $70.2 million was set for 2012–13, pro-rated to a 48-game schedule. The cap for 2013–14 was set at $64.3 million, while the floor was set at $44 million. The salary cap cannot go below $64.3 million for the life of the current CBA, which will run for ten years, ending with the 2021–22 NHL season. Starting with the 2014–15 season, the salary cap will be based on a 50/50 revenue split between players and teams. These are the basic rules. In fact, the NHL salary cap system is highly complex and will be looked at in more detail in subsequent chapters of this book. (The NBA also has a hard cap system now, but with many quirky exceptions that allow teams to exceed the cap.)

Major League Baseball still does not have a hard salary cap. Instead of a hard cap, MLB has a "luxury tax" that is paid when the player payroll exceeds a pre-negotiated amount—$178 million in 2013, which will rise to $189 million in 2014. This amount is far beyond the revenue-generating capacity of nearly every team in MLB. Such a high level reflects both the negotiating skills of the players association and the high level of influence possessed by a few powerful franchises, led by the New York Yankees. (This aspect will also be examined in greater detail later in the book.)

Revenue Sharing

If a league wants to create a more level playing field among its franchises, one of the fundamental steps it can take is to implement a system in which a significant portion of league-wide revenues are shared among its teams. The relationship between revenue sharing and competitiveness within the league is simple: the more that revenue is shared among the teams, the more the playing field is levelled—financially and competitively. In fact, leagues were created in the first place to foster fair competition among teams by imposing a uniform set of rules—so revenue sharing is aligned philosophically with the concept of a sports league.

The easiest revenue sources to share are those that are earned by the league as a whole—such as fees from national broadcasting and related media, collective merchandising, all-star games or similar league-wide events, or revenues related to special events, such as the NHL's participation in the Olympics. Fees from league expansion are another significant potential source of shared revenue (and, over the years, have created a bias in favour of expansion).

Convincing successful teams that they should share revenues from such things as sales of tickets, food and drink, team merchandise, and local broadcast rights is much more difficult. Teams can argue that their own-source revenue is the result of their own marketing and sales efforts in their home market—and they should not have to share it with teams that have not done as good a job at boosting revenue. But the counter-argument is that if there was no opponent on the field to face these successful franchises, there would be no fans to buy the tickets, food and drink, and merchandise. Therefore, there is a basic logic to sharing at least some of these revenues among all franchises. In fact, implicit revenue sharing also occurs when the more popular teams with wide fan bases (such as the Red Sox, Maple Leafs, or Lakers) visit an opponent and attract additional fans to the game.

A league's approach to revenue sharing says a great deal about the underlying business philosophy of the league. The NFL leads the way in terms of advancing the collective business interests of the league. Other leagues have adopted the opposite philosophy—every man for himself and minimal sharing of revenues. In those leagues, revenue sharing only becomes an interesting idea when financial weakness in some franchises begins to threaten the local revenues or franchise values of the financially strong teams.

The relationship between revenue sharing and competitiveness within the league is simple: the more that revenue is shared among the teams, the more the playing field is levelled—financially and competitively.

The NFL has set the standard when it comes to revenue sharing. For decades, the NFL and its franchises have shared more than 80 per cent of league and club revenues—a great example of putting the collective interest ahead of the individual team interest (although some maverick owners, such as Jerry Jones in Dallas and Al Davis in Oakland, have shown they are only too happy to seize opportunities to make more money outside of the league-sharing formula). Television broadcast revenues for the NFL are currently worth $5 billion annually and are shared evenly among all franchises, as are merchandising revenues. To ensure that it has an attractive product for TV, the NFL has placed considerable weight on establishing a competitive balance on the field, and most analysts agree that the NFL is the leader in that regard. Not surprisingly, the NFL is the most prosperous pro sports league in North America, with over half the franchises valued by *Forbes* at $1 billion or more. In this case, there appears to be a relationship between the league's competitive conditions and the financial results.

The on-again, off-again, on-again NFL player lockout that occurred in 2011 was an indication of the stakes involved in sharing the massive revenues of the league. But it also signalled the risks to the NFL's revenue-generating capacity when common sense in labour relations does not prevail.

The NHL's revenue-sharing system is based on a different business philosophy. The NHL has a TV revenue pool that has increased to about US$600 million annually (shared among its 30 franchises, or about $20 million per team), thanks to a 10-year deal with NBC in the U.S. and a 12-year-deal with Rogers in Canada. But individual teams are free to develop their own independent TV deals for games not covered in the national/regional TV packages. So if the NHL decided to extend its revenue sharing, the additional money would have to be pulled out of the individual teams' pockets—a key difference from the NFL's collective approach. Since the money would be coming directly from their own coffers, owners of the more successful NHL franchises have a good reason to share only as much revenue as is necessary to keep the weakest franchises from collapsing and thereby depressing the value of the surviving franchises.

Access to Player Talent

Common, or comparable, access to player talent across the league is another way of creating a more level playing field among franchises.

The market for player talent has come a long way from the early days of pro sports when the competition for talent was little more than a free-for-all. Decades ago, depending on the sport, a team could gain a competitive advantage on the field or rink by creating a competitive advantage in spotting talent. A team could:

- develop a deep knowledge of its local market (as the Montreal Canadiens did, which led to their historical dominance in the francophone Quebec talent pool);
- search out talent in distant markets (as some baseball teams did in Latin America); or
- use a cozy relationship with feeder teams to protect and groom certain players (such as we still see in the soccer world with its academy system).

In today's player talent market, the playing field is much more level. The first step in bringing some order and fairness to the market for player talent was to introduce a common selection process, or "entry draft," for young talent. This practice emerged during the 1950s and 1960s, depending on the sports league. The entry draft system sets common rules under which teams can acquire young players. These rules generally include a minimum age at which a player can be drafted, and can also include such conditions as past experience and the geographical region in which a team has precedence. The draft system prevents teams from hoarding new talent. And by having the weakest teams pick first and the strongest last (based on the team standings in the preceding season), the entry draft gives the weaker teams preferential access to the expected best new talent—thereby making the league more competitive.

The next significant step in expanding access to player talent was the gradual introduction of free agency for existing players. Baseball was a trendsetter here. Names like Curt Flood, Andy Messersmith, and Dave McNally immediately come to mind as pioneers in the fight against the "reserve clause"[1] and champions of free-agent status once an existing contract with a specific team had expired.

The market for player talent has come a long way from the early days of pro sports when the competition for talent was little more than a free-for-all.

To a great extent, all the major pro sports leagues have now adopted the same operating model—a common, reverse-order draft and free agency for players who have reached a certain level of seniority or who meet other conditions. The specific details of the entry draft and free agency vary considerably among the pro sports leagues

1   The reserve clause was included in every MLB contract. It stated that the team retained the sole right to the player's services even after the contract expired—effectively binding that player to the team forever, or until the team decided to trade or release him. The clause was abolished in 1975.

and are inevitably at the centre of the players associations' contract negotiations with the leagues. As we've already noted, MLB does not have a hard salary cap. And the lack of a cap means that the richest teams are free to outbid the others in the battle to sign the top free agents—which undermines the role of free agency in levelling the MLB playing field.

Globalization has also become a factor of growing importance for the professional team sports that have international appeal and a corresponding international talent pool. Soccer is the most globalized team sport. Team rosters in many leagues, including North America's MLS, are made up of players from around the world. In recent years, some top teams in the top English soccer league (the "Premiership") have fielded full squads of eleven with not a single English player on the pitch. North American pro sports leagues are not immune to the forces of globalization. They have quickly internationalized their talent base. Baseball was first, followed by hockey and basketball. The globalization of talent is a circular, or symbiotic, process. As the various team sports have grown in global popularity, more and more talented players have begun to emerge in many new regions. The North American pro sports leagues have responded by searching for and hiring these talented athletes from outside North America—which, in turn, helps to further fuel the global popularity of the sport.

Changes in Competitive Conditions

Changes in the specific competitive conditions within a league can also play a major role in the success or failure of franchises. As discussed in Chapter 2, changes in the exchange rate can be particularly important for franchises in leagues that operate in more than one country.

Another factor that can influence the competitive conditions is the relative tax burden imposed in the various markets. If a team is located in a market where the personal income tax rate is higher than elsewhere in the league, or where there are any special or local taxes applied to high-income professional athletes, that team will be relatively less attractive to free agents. Higher rates of taxation can also reduce the purchasing power of individual consumers and limit their ability to buy tickets. The same logic applies to business taxation affecting the franchise. A relatively higher rate of business taxation would constrain the profitability—and therefore the competitiveness— of an individual franchise, as would a reduced ability for client businesses to write off the costs of such expenses as corporate boxes.

Conversely, tax advantages can also be created to encourage free agents to consider a specific market, or to provide an incentive for individuals or businesses to support pro sports through ticket purchases, corporate box rentals, and advertising.

Conclusion

Most sports fans believe that creating a level playing field among the franchises in a given league is a noble and worthy goal. After all, who could object to the idea of giving every team a fair chance—based only on effort, teamwork, leadership, and management skill—to win the championship every year? Isn't that the raison d'être for sports?

But in practice, a level playing field among the franchises in a given league can be elusive. Pro sport leagues have made some advances in establishing a level playing field, but these advances are often selective and reflect the league's underlying business model and the balance of power within the league.

The "level playing field" concept is applied by most leagues—at least to some degree—when it comes to access to player talent. The results include such things as an entry draft, free agency, and the creation of a salary cap. But the concept is much less likely to be applied to the same degree when it comes to revenue sharing.

How far a league goes in implementing a level playing field among its franchises often says a great deal about the distribution of economic power within that league. And sports fans who eagerly hand over their money—and their hearts—to their favourite team should keep in mind the fact that the underlying competitive conditions are not always equal.

Chapter 4
Why Pro Sports Franchises Succeed … and Fail

Most pro sports leagues are built around the same business model—individual owners acquire a franchise giving them the right to operate a team within the league. So why, then, do some pro sports franchises succeed while others languish?

In the previous chapters of this book, we defined the pro sports market in Canada, identified four market pillars for success, and examined league competitive conditions. When the fundamental market and league conditions are right, a pro sports franchise can be very successful.

But as we have seen time and again, franchise success is hardly guaranteed. There can be huge differences in financial and competitive performance among franchises. In this chapter, we assess the franchise-specific factors that determine whether a professional sports franchise—which is, after all, a business—will succeed in a given community.

Certain key factors can make a good franchise great or, conversely, can undermine a franchise that enjoys otherwise strong market and league conditions. The factors examined here are:

- ownership and management strength;
- the availability of adequate playing facilities;
- fan support for the team.

Ownership and Management Strength

A key to team success—both athletically (on the field or rink) and financially (off the field)—is the strength of the franchise's ownership and management. Two franchises in the same league can have similar market pillars, yet achieve widely different competitive and financial results over time—and, in most cases, the quality of ownership and management will prove to be the key difference.

Each pro sports franchise has a mixture of ownership, business management, and team management. In terms of ownership, franchises can be owned by corporate entities (such as MLSE, which owns the Maple Leafs, Raptors, and Toronto FC); by a group of owners; or by an individual. The ownership helps to establish the "business culture" of the franchise—and, specifically, the balance between financial results and competitive performance. Some owners are prepared to make massive financial investments in their team in an effort to attain a competitive advantage wherever possible within the operating conditions of the league. Financial results are a secondary concern. Some are concerned principally with financial results, requiring only a performance on the field that is adequate to keep the fans interested. Others impose a spending limit on the management of the team, which is often a sign that the team is on a downward spiral.

The franchise ownership normally hires a management team that runs the franchise as a business but also works to ensure that the team is competitive within the given pro sports league. Key positions in franchise management include a team president, who oversees all business operations; a general manager, who, under the budget provided by the owner and president, seeks out the players that will make the team as competitive as possible; and a head coach, who provides daily guidance to the athletes. (Team competitive performance is a shared responsibility, but the coach is often the fall guy when a team fails to win enough.)

Many different combinations of ownership, franchise business management, and team management can be identified among pro sports franchises. For example, some owners meddle deeply in team affairs, even acting as the team's general manager. Some teams combine the general manager and head coach positions, making one person responsible for both the selection of player talent and the team's day-to-day performance. The sports media are filled with stories about the mixture of ownership, management, and coaching and the effects on the teams' results on the field.

Chronically weak franchise management and poor decision-making can, over time, create a self-perpetuating cycle of mediocrity and steady decline. Continued underperformance—such as missing the playoffs year after year—feeds dissatisfaction among the fan base. Fewer fans buy tickets to games or tune in to media broadcasts, which means less money coming in for the franchise. In a bid to remain profitable or to limit losses, the player payroll is reduced. A smaller payroll makes it harder for the team to attract and retain the talent it needs to improve its performance on the field or rink—which further feeds dissatisfaction among the fan base.

There are many cases of pro sports franchises operating in strong business markets but fielding perennially weak teams. These cases may reflect local market conditions, poor ownership and management, or a combination of both.

If this cycle is not broken (such as by a change in ownership or management, and/or through brilliant drafting and development of top talent), it will likely lead eventually to the failure of the franchise. The Ottawa Rough Riders stand as a textbook example of a combined ownership-management failure. The franchise, which dated back to

1876, fielded losing teams through most of the 1980s and into the 1990s. The resulting downward spiral only came to an end in 1996 when the franchise folded.

In contrast, the Chicago Blackhawks are a great example of a turnaround in pro sports ownership and management. In 2004, ESPN named the Blackhawks, under long-time owner Bill Wirtz, the worst franchise in pro sports. After Bill Wirtz's death in 2007, his son Rocky assumed control of the team and began modernizing its business practices—including finally allowing home games to be broadcast on local television. Astute drafting, which brought young stars such as Jonathan Toews, Patrick Kane, and Duncan Keith to the Windy City, was another important management factor. Finishing near the bottom of the standings for so many years gave the team a higher position in the entry draft, but that advantage would have meant nothing if management had failed to make the right selections on draft day. Thanks to many right moves by ownership and management, the Hawks went from half-empty stands and failure to qualify for the playoffs as recently as 2008, to sellouts and Stanley Cup championships in 2010 and 2013. What was the key ingredient that led to the remarkably rapid turnaround? In the case of the Chicago Blackhawks, it was clearly the change to the team's ownership and management.

To a lesser extent, the Boston Bruins are also an example of how a good franchise can become a champion through better management. After years of being a perennial contender, the Bruins fell off in the late 1990s and actually failed to make the playoffs in 2006 and 2007. In the strong New England sports market, where many of the other major pro sports had all had championship teams in recent years, the Bruins became something of an afterthought. But changes in management—demonstrated through skilled free agent signings (notably defenceman Zdeno Chara), trades, and drafting—helped the Bruins win the Stanley Cup in 2011, their first championship in 39 years, and reach the Cup final again in 2013.

While the success of most businesses is measured purely by their financial performance, sports franchises have an added measure of success—their won-lost record on the playing field. There are, of course, many cases of pro sports franchises operating in strong business markets but fielding perennially weak teams. These cases may reflect local market conditions that allow the team to draw well without having much competitive success, or they may be the result of poor ownership and management, or some combination thereof.

The Chicago Cubs may represent the most striking case of sustained failure on the field, yet a continuing success at the box office. All the other factors we identify in this book work to the Cubs' advantage—the four market pillars, league conditions, and a historic playing facility. Yet, despite playing to full houses and regularly having one of the top payrolls in Major League Baseball, the Cubs have not won a World Series since 1908. Elsewhere, the National Hockey League's New York Rangers are able to play each home game to a sold-out house at Madison Square Garden and boast a roster that lists some of the NHL's highest-paid players—yet the Rangers have won precisely one Stanley Cup since 1941. Many of the same conditions exist for sports franchises in Toronto, where financial success has not been matched by sustained success on the field or on the ice in recent years. (The Argonauts' success in winning the Grey Cup in 2012 was an exception, not the norm.)

We know that financial conditions affect the overall performance of governments and firms. In the case of pro sports, questionable financial decisions by ownership can clearly affect the results on the field as well. The English soccer club Liverpool FC provides a recent example of how ownership, financial management, and team performance are interlinked. In 2007, American businessmen George Gillett and Tom Hicks purchased the club, relying heavily on financial leveraging to complete the deal. They quickly found themselves financially overextended, and they nearly destroyed Liverpool FC's premium brand before selling the club to another U.S.-based group in 2010.

Pro Sports Facilities

To be competitive, a sports franchise needs an appropriate stadium or arena—one that will pull in the fans who pay to watch their sports heroes in action.

The question of who should pay for new sports facilities to be used by professional teams and athletes is a hot topic of public debate and will be examined in a later chapter. In an ideal world, both the pro sports franchise and its playing facility would be privately financed and would operate profitably. Unfortunately, things seldom work out perfectly in the real world. It is likely that only a handful of Canadian markets are large enough to allow a pro sports facility to operate profitably as a private venture. Many governments, therefore, face recurring requests and public pressure to provide some form of public financial support for pro sports facilities. These facilities can provide quality-of-life and other benefits to the community as a whole, especially if governments make use of well-designed financing and governance structures to minimize the financial impact on the public purse. The economic costs and benefits to the community—and to society as a whole—of providing public support for a new facility should be evaluated in order to bring substance to the public debate.

> Baseball's brand is particularly tied to tradition while pro football's brand is firmly rooted in the here and now.

To succeed financially, a professional sports team must have a playing facility that is competitive in terms of scale and quality with the rest of the league. The idea of what constitutes appropriate scale and quality for a sports facility has slowly evolved over the years as real incomes have risen and as some pro sports franchises have seen their popularity soar while others in the same city or region watched their popularity fade. Baseball's brand is particularly tied to tradition, and some ancient ballparks are part of that brand. Aged facilities such as Fenway Park in Boston or Wrigley Field in Chicago lack many modern features but are revered for their history. Yankee Stadium was also part of that baseball brand, but the Yankee ownership decided that the benefits of a storied facility were outweighed by the advantages of a new one. The Yankees successfully managed a transition from an old stadium to a new one while keeping the brand of tradition and history alive. Over the past 20 years, many other MLB ballparks—from Baltimore, Maryland, to Arlington, Texas—have combined traditional features or "looks" at their ballparks with modern amenities.

Pro football has its history, too. But its brand is firmly rooted in the here and now—and so are its playing facilities. The newest NFL facilities—such as Cowboy Stadium, home to the Dallas Cowboys and the 2011 Super Bowl—were built to a massive scale (room for 100,000-plus spectators), with price tags to match ($1.15 billion in the case of Dallas), and have every client-friendly amenity imaginable, and then some. The playing facilities for Canadian Football League teams are steadily being upgraded, while the NHL has seen revered historic buildings, such as Maple Leaf Gardens and the Montreal Forum, replaced by larger and more financially lucrative buildings that include more corporate boxes, restaurants, and other places where fans can spend their money. Like the Yankees, the Montreal Canadiens and Toronto Maple Leafs managed successful transitions from revered but aging buildings to modern state-of-the-art facilities without upsetting their fan base.

Fan Support for the Team

The third factor for franchise success is what economists refer to as "consumer taste"—which, in this context, means the evolving appeal of specific pro sports to the consumer.

What determines the appeal of a specific pro sport to a specific local community? We are not marketing experts or sociologists, but our experience as professional economists and our passion for sports allow us to identify some of the top-line factors that can influence fan support for a team.

Tradition and History

The first and most important factor is local tradition and history. Hockey is popular in Canada because it is part of our national culture. Hockey was created in Canada; it has been part of Canadian winter recreation since the mid-19th century. Hockey is a natural sport of choice in a land covered by ice and snow for up to six months of the year. If you were born in Canada, hockey is a part of your identity—whether you played it or not. Even if you weren't born here, hockey has its appeals. It is fast-paced and (unlike North American football) easy to understand. And hockey talk is everywhere—from the evening newscasts to the water cooler at work. The multitude of minor hockey organizations and multi-level junior leagues gives hockey a strong local presence in even the smallest of Canadian communities. And the development of multiple, highly competitive TV sports channels has strengthened the profile and distribution of pro hockey in Canada. With this foundation in place, pro hockey is an easy sell in Canadian communities from coast to coast, which is why there is perpetual debate about whether Canada could sustain more NHL franchises.

The success of a pro sports franchise is driven by many factors, notably ownership and management, the home facility in which the franchise plays, and the degree and intensity of fan support.

The story is very different in the southern United States. Hockey's history there is limited. Kids in the suburbs of the South don't play hockey on the streets; they shoot hoops in the driveway. Snowstorms are seen as an aberration to be abhorred, not a natural cycle to be embraced (or at least tolerated and managed). Moreover, the NHL has not succeeded in attracting season-long, significant national TV coverage, a problem that limits its ability to market the game to a national U.S. audience. With such a limited local tradition and so little national media exposure, it is hardly a surprise that Atlanta moved to Winnipeg in the spring of 2011 and that other NHL franchises based in the southern U.S. are struggling—in some cases, after 20 or more years of strong local marketing efforts to sell the game. We don't know what the future holds for hockey in the southern U.S., but the list of challenged southern NHL franchises is long.

Globalization

When it comes to building or maintaining fan support for sports franchises, the forces of globalization can work against local factors such as tradition and history. Globalization has created channels for the global distribution of popular culture and entertainment. Soccer immediately comes to mind as the pro team sport that is most globalized in terms of branding, merchandizing, and media coverage. And not surprisingly, its popularity is rising in Canada. Pro soccer's growth in this country is being propelled by significant grassroots participation and by more media exposure globally and locally. But this growth also reflects an increasingly diverse population. Many new Canadians bring their love for soccer with them when they come to Canada. That "taste" for soccer is being transferred to Canada, which now has Major League Soccer franchises in Toronto, Montréal, and Vancouver. As local interest in soccer grows, fan loyalty for a specific pro soccer team can be developed remarkably quickly. Other pro team sports that have gone global (though not as dramatically as soccer) include basketball, hockey, rugby, baseball, and cricket. As well, many individual pro sports—such as golf, tennis, auto racing, track and field, boxing, and even mixed martial arts—are also popular today around the globe.

Marketing Power

A third factor influencing the success of a franchise is the marketing of the sport or league as a whole, both locally and nationally. In the United States, pro football is the leader when it comes to marketing its product. Over the past four decades, the National Football League has built a remarkable brand. The first Super Bowl was played in 1967—and the stadium was not sold out. It has since become the most important event on the North American pro sports calendar, far surpassing baseball's World Series and other league championships. Another key marketing move saw the NFL break away from the tradition of overlapping Sunday afternoon games, which it did by staggering start times and by pushing NFL games into prime time on TV with the launch of Monday Night Football in 1970 (and later on with Thursday and Sunday night games).

Another example of the marketing savvy of the NFL is the way it repackages its own product. The NFL relies heavily upon its in-house service, NFL Films, to build the imagery of football and make it widely available to the public. By producing its own programming, the NFL makes its product available throughout the year, including the league's off-season. And slow-motion filming using multiple cameras, combined with dramatic music, creates a larger-than-life aura of the game for NFL football fans old and new.

To support the NFL marketing machine, the on-field product itself is in a constant state of evolution, with rule changes designed to generate more offence and scoring, thereby making the game more exciting to fans.

Demographics

A fourth factor driving fan support is demographics. Demographics influence which sports the kids choose to watch (and play). The disposable income levels of various demographic groups also affect sports choices. A detailed comparison of pro sport popularity by demographic group is beyond the scope of this book but would provide some revealing insights. A comparison of the demographics of baseball fans versus that of basketball fans, for example, would be particularly interesting, since our casual observation is that basketball today is attracting an ethnically diverse and young following in a way that baseball can only look upon with envy.

Conclusion

The success of a pro sports franchise, financially and competitively, is driven by many factors. So far in this book, we have outlined the four market pillars for success, examined league competitive conditions, and have now added three factors specific to franchises.

The first is franchise ownership and management. Two franchises in the same league can have similar market pillars, yet achieve widely different competitive and financial results over time due to the quality of ownership and the management hired to run the team.

Next is the home facility in which the franchise plays. While there are some aging baseball facilities that are revered for their tradition, most successful franchises prefer a modern facility that maximizes the fan experience—and the cash flow.

The third and final franchise success factor is fan support. We have identified and examined briefly four elements of fan support—local tradition and history, globalization, marketing power, and demographics—as key factors that determine the degree and intensity of fan support for a given team.

Chapter 5
Who Should Pay for
New Pro Sports Facilities?

Big-league teams need big-league facilities. But today's big-league facilities can easily cost $400 million or more to build. And deciding who will foot the bill inevitably leads to controversy.

The question of who should pay for new sports facilities to be used by professional teams and athletes is a frequent and hot topic of public debate. The specific issue is whether, when, and how governments should help to pay for new pro sports facilities. This issue has economic, financial, and socio-political dimensions—and there is no single right answer.

The Economic Dimension

The main purpose of a new pro sports facility is to allow a franchise and its owner(s) to be viable—that is, the facility is intended to help the private investors in the franchise make money, or at least break even. In an ideal world, pro sports franchises and their facilities would be both privately financed and profitable. Of course, things often don't work out perfectly in the real world. But a reasonable starting point for deciding whether to build any new pro sports facility would be to assess the conditions under which it could be privately financed, with investors in the facility making a profit from its construction and operation. In some cases, the economic evaluation may be positive, and the facility could then be built solely with private capital.

The Air Canada Centre (ACC) in Toronto is one of those cases. Although the financial structure was very convoluted and "creative" (including a mid-construction change in ownership in 1998 and a redesign of the facility itself), the ACC was built with private financing, thanks to a remarkably high degree of corporate sponsorship.[1] As well, the ACC was built on land in downtown Toronto that was acquired from Canada Post at what was reported to be an exceptionally low price— well below its market value.[2] A direct public contribution—reportedly valued at $13 million and related to infrastructure financing—was provided in the late 1990s. Ever since, the ACC's underlying economics have remained strong, since it hosts a significant number of events (up to 200 annually), each of which generates rental income and other earnings.

The Bell Centre in Montréal and Rogers Arena in Vancouver were also privately financed. The fact that these three arenas (with financially successful NHL teams as their principal tenants) were privately financed indicates that the right economic conditions for pro sports facilities to be privately financed can exist in large urban centres in Canada. (The renamed Canadian Tire Centre in Ottawa was also privately financed, but went through bankruptcy proceedings. It was acquired by the current owner for a fraction of the construction costs.)

However, not all pro sports facilities, and not all communities, enjoy comparable strength in terms of private financial capacity for construction, maintenance, and operation. The size of the local market may be too small; there may be only a limited number of events that could use the facility and pay rent; and/or there may be insufficient private sector appetite for risk-taking, or inadequate local and national corporate sponsorship. At that point, other questions can be posed about whether there are any economic benefits to society from making available some form of public financial support for the facility.

---

1   See theaircanadacentre.com for chronological details on ownership and sponsorship.

2   See Stevie Cameron's book *On the Take: Crime Corruption and Greed in the Mulroney Years* (Toronto: Seal Books, 1995) for one account of how the ACC's land was acquired.

Professional sports facilities can have attributes of what economists call "public goods"—that is, they provide economic benefits to society as a whole, and not just to the franchise owners, athletes, and fans. For example, a new pro sports facility and the franchise or franchises that use it might help to raise the profile of a community as a place for private investors to locate. The facility could encourage local entrepreneurs to create new ventures, or it could draw in tourists. All these things would bring ongoing economic benefits to the community. The facility can be used for other for-profit events (such as concerts), but also by amateur athletes or for other socially oriented purposes (for example, blood donation clinics or charity fundraising events), which might increase the possible benefit to all of society. The economic benefits to the community and to society as a whole can be evaluated, as can the costs, using techniques that economists have developed over many years.

From a purely economic perspective, there is not a compelling case for public sector investment in pro sports facilities. But other considerations need to be examined.

Vancouver, B.C., and Canada certainly reaped global "marquee" benefits during the 2010 Winter Olympics, which could pay off in terms of increasing tourism and attracting more foreign investment, thereby offsetting at least part of the cost to taxpayers of developing the many Olympic facilities. Conversely, a public investment project that turns out badly can bring unwanted negative publicity to a community and negatively influence investor and visitor perceptions. The economic impact of the 1976 Montréal Olympics on the local economy is still a subject of debate, particularly given the recurring structural and financial problems of the Olympic Stadium (or "The Big Owe" to some of us) and the allegations of corrupt financial practices during its construction.

In addition, positive economic benefits are likely to result from the investment, and these can be estimated. The dollars spent on labour and capital for the specific investment—and its ongoing operations—get re-spent in the local economy, creating multiplier effects, such as increased wages and additional jobs. But there are also bound to be significant economic costs and "leakages" from a pro sports project, including interest costs on borrowed public money, or imports used in construction and operation. A proper evaluation would need to consider whether the investment in a new professional sports facility was creating new or "incremental" activity, or simply displacing private or public investment that would have occurred in the community in any event. Governments need to consider alternative public infrastructure programs that might also generate economic and social benefits for the same funding. Public money needs to be spent wisely.

This means assessing what economists call the "opportunity costs"—a key variable in any kind of cost-benefit analysis (although challenging to assess). In the context of public money for professional sports facilities, opportunity costs mean that if a stadium or arena requires, say, $400 million in public investment, the alternative use for these public funds needs to be examined as well. If detailed economic analysis indicates that a similar investment of $400 million on other kinds of activities would yield stronger overall benefits to society, then the government should move forward with that other project, not with the stadium or arena.

In general, the economic literature indicates that publicly financed pro sports facilities do not create positive net economic benefits for the community. While positive benefits can and do exist, there are also significant economic costs associated with such projects; the public money used to construct and operate the facility is supported by the tax base and is often diverted from other uses in the local economy. From a purely economic perspective, therefore, there is not a compelling case for public sector investment in pro sports facilities. But there are other dimensions to consider.

The Financial Dimension

The financial dimension—the financial costs of private and/or public investment in sports facilities, and the revenue benefits—must be considered in detail. Many pro sports facilities utilize a blend of private and public financing, from multiple sources, in order to make the project a reality.

Let's focus specifically on possible public sector support. There will be a direct financial cost to a government if money is borrowed to make the investment, with required regular payments of interest and the repayment of principal. If money is taken from the current budget to pay for a new sports facility, then other government priorities will not be financed and will have to be postponed or cancelled, or additional revenues will have to be raised.

The financial impact on governments can also be indirect, such as in the case of a government guarantee in whole or in part that is provided to help raise private financing. This indirect financial impact is called a "contingent liability" for the government. Appropriate government accounting practices would put a price on these contingent liabilities within a government's books—assessing the risk of the guarantee actually being used, and the estimated cost. Complex financial techniques are now applied to most projects, including sports facilities, designed to manage the financial costs and related implications for all investors and guarantors.

Numerous financial management options exist, including making use of private-public partnerships (or PPPs), which are increasingly being used in Canada and around the world.

On the positive side of the financial ledger, governments derive revenues from public investment in sports facilities. Tax revenues can be generated from the facility itself, from the franchise's operations, and from the salaries of the athletes and other employees. Income taxes on player salaries (which for some athletes are in the millions) can be a particularly valuable and ongoing source of revenue. Special taxes on the salaries of visiting players have been levied in a few locations to increase the local tax revenue from pro sports. Of course, in Canada, it is the federal and provincial/territorial governments that levy income taxes, not cities—which may be a reason for opening the discussion around the role of more senior levels of government in public investment in pro sports facilities.

In recent years, the selling of naming rights for publicly financed facilities (and private ones, too) have become a very popular way of generating additional revenue from the facility, helping to cover a portion of the capital and operating costs. Of the 30 arenas that host NHL teams, only three older facilities—Joe Louis Arena in Detroit, Madison Square Garden in Manhattan, and Nassau Veterans Memorial Coliseum on Long Island—have not sold naming rights to businesses. The annual cash flow produced by the sale of naming rights varies considerably by facility and tends to be in the range of $2 million to $4 million annually. These naming rights are usually sold after the facility has been constructed, so the construction costs and risks are borne by public and private sector financiers.

We would also emphasize that direct budgetary support by governments for all or some of the construction of a new pro sports facility is not the only way to proceed. Other operating and governance structures can be created as means of building confidence that the benefits will be maximized and the costs and risks minimized. Numerous financial management options exist, including making use of private-public partnerships (or PPPs), which are increasingly being used in Canada and around the world. For example, a pro sports facility project could be designed so that the private sector assumes the risks and costs of construction and operation of the facility for a period of time, and then eventually transfers control of the property back to the government. An arm's-length management entity could be created to oversee public investment in a specific pro sports facility and to manage the performance. Or a pro sports facility could be developed and financed by the private sector, but with selective guarantees provided by the public sector for specific risks related to construction and operation. All of the options need to be considered as means of minimizing the direct and indirect financial impacts on the public sector.

The Political Dimension

The politics of possible public investment in pro sports facilities can be fascinating. Is public expenditure in a specific pro sports facility a high priority for the community? Specifically, would it improve the perceived "quality of life" for those living in the community and make people happier and more engaged citizens? Those are questions for each community to decide, through its own political process. Some communities may decide that having a pro sports franchise is so important to the community (due to its impact on its image, its culture, and/or its economy) that they will accept the financial costs and risks of building a new facility. Of course, other communities may reach a different view about the trade-off between what are generally the net economic costs of public financial support for a new facility and the perceived quality of life benefits.

Many citizens in Winnipeg today believe that the quality of life in their community has been enhanced by the return of an NHL franchise. There is an added bonus in that the arena where the Jets will play was largely financed with private money. Similarly, many citizens in Québec City believe that the quality of life in their community would be improved by the return of an NHL franchise— which is why they elected a mayor who clearly supports public investment in a new arena that would meet today's NHL standards and would help attract a team back to Québec City. The project is, indeed, becoming a reality. And by 2015, a new, publicly funded, NHL-ready facility will be open for business in Québec City.

> Governments would need to demonstrate the benefit of using significant public funds to finance the construction of a pro sports facility or facilities.

Another question: Is it possible to reap some positive financial or economic returns from public expenditure on a new facility, giving it some attributes of an investment? Or would the construction of a new facility simply be a form of mass consumption, with the taxpayer absorbing many of the costs of construction and even ongoing operations? Again, some solid economic and financial analysis could be used to help guide the discussion through the political process.

With three levels of government in Canada (federal, provincial/territorial, and municipal), the politics of government involvement in new pro sports facilities, and the related economic impacts and finances, can be highly complex and will vary considerably among possible projects and jurisdictions. In general, there is probably a stronger economic, financial, and political case for local levels of government to invest in pro sports facilities, since most of the expected social benefits and any economic benefits would be reaped locally. More senior levels of government, or those responsible for larger jurisdictions, would have to take issues such as fairness and a level playing field across the jurisdictions more fully into account—particularly if there are requests for investment assistance from multiple cities and multiple sports.

Each government's overall fiscal capacity also needs to be considered. The recession of 2008–09 resulted in large fiscal deficits and higher public debt loads at both the federal and provincial levels. As a result, even more than before, governments need to demonstrate the benefit of using significant public funds to finance the construction of a pro sports facility or facilities. This is particularly true at the political level, since these facilities will be used by professional athletes earning multi-million-dollar annual salaries for, in most cases, the benefit of multi-millionaire franchise owners. Moreover, given the current tight fiscal framework for most governments, cutbacks elsewhere may be required in order to make an investment in pro sports facilities.

Putting It All Together

Validating public investment in pro sports facilities is challenging, but it is not an impossible task. Governments most certainly should do their homework on the possible socio-economic benefits to the community—and come up with financial structures that make sense economically, financially, and politically—if they are to build and maintain public support for the investment. No two communities, facilities, or investment proposals are identical, so each would have to be assessed based on its own economic, financial, and political merits. The Conference Board of Canada uses its analytical tools regularly for clients, estimating the economic impacts and evaluating the financial and fiscal dimensions of a given project or proposal.

In general, local and state governments in the United States have shown a willingness to provide public support for new pro sports facilities. In Nashville, for example, the arena used by the NHL's Predators cost $144 million to build in the mid-1990s and was financed entirely by the City of Nashville through a general bond issue. Subsequently, naming rights have been sold sequentially to various corporations as a way to offset the bond payments by the city.

This apparent willingness of U.S. cities and states to pay for facilities in whole or in part may reflect to a large degree the intensity of interest in multiple pro sports in the U.S. and the high degree of rivalry between and among cities. Often that support is provided by making subsidized financing available—such as through tax-free municipal bonds. But numerous other forms of concessions are also utilized, limited only by the imagination of the financiers and beneficiaries.

If governments are to reap the maximum benefits from any investment in a facility at the lowest cost possible, they need to do their homework before making commitments.

However, fiscal circumstances in the U.S. have changed. The ongoing fiscal mess at all three levels of government will last for years to come, and will constrain the ability of governments at any level to provide future funding for facilities.

Conclusion

In an ideal world, pro sports franchises and their playing facilities would both be privately financed and operate profitably. The facilities used by NHL teams in Montréal, Toronto, and Vancouver were constructed using private financing—which indicates that in large urban centres in Canada, the right economic conditions can exist for pro sports facilities to be privately financed. But for other facilities and in other communities, there may be constraints in terms of market size or limits to the private sector's risk-taking and financial capacity. Governments therefore face recurring requests and public pressure to provide some form of public financial support for professional sports facilities if the community is to attract or retain a pro sports team.

In general, the economic literature indicates that publicly financed pro sports facilities do not create positive net economic benefits for the community. However, those facilities could enhance the quality of life in the community and provide socio-economic benefits to society as a whole, especially if governments make use of strong economic analysis and well-designed financing and governance structures to minimize the economic and financial costs to the community. The socio-economic benefits and costs to the community and to society as a whole can be evaluated using techniques that economists have developed over many years.

Canadian governments are not immune to the pressures to finance new pro sports facilities. If they are to reap the maximum benefits from any investment in a facility at the lowest cost possible, governments need to do their homework—assessing carefully the economic, financial, and political dimensions and establishing a credible governance structure—before making commitments. (Hopefully, Québec City mayor Régis Labeaume did exactly that before moving forward in the fall of 2012 with the building of a new NHL-ready arena.)

Chapter 6
Pro League Competitive Conditions and How the NHL Stacks Up

All the major pro sports leagues pay lip service to the concept of ensuring a "level playing field." But while all "talk the talk," there is a wide disparity among the leagues when it comes to "walking the walk." In this chapter, we look at what the NHL and its rivals have done to make their leagues more competitive.

In Chapter 3, we looked at the mechanisms that leagues use to create a "level playing field" among their teams. Clearly, the more level the playing field, the more competitive—and compelling—the league is for its fans. In this chapter, we look at the competitive conditions among the National Hockey League's biggest North American competitors— Major League Baseball (MLB), the National Football League (NFL), and the National Basketball Association (NBA). And we look at how the NHL compares with its rivals.

Salary Caps and Player Salaries

Most professional sports leagues today have some form of salary cap. Caps are designed to allow all franchises to operate profitably. In an era of free agency, a cap constrains the ability of players (or more specifically, their agents) to bid up salaries to levels at which only a handful of clubs can afford to sign the top players. Since no team can grossly outspend its competitors when it comes to player payrolls, a salary cap also helps to level the competitive playing field among teams, which appeals to the fan base. All four of the top North American leagues have caps based on a division of revenues between the teams and the players, and all regularly face the risk that their players will strike to back their demands for a great share of those revenues.

The NFL, the NHL, and the NBA have "hard" salary caps, with firm upper limits on annual player salaries. In the case of the NBA, the system includes an array of significant and arcane exemptions that can allow teams to exceed the defined cap. Major League Baseball does not have a hard cap, but it does have "soft" salary caps.

> In an era of free agency, a cap constrains the ability of players to bid up salaries to levels at which only a handful of clubs can afford to sign the top players.

We will examine the NHL salary cap system in detail later. In this chapter, we focus on Major League Baseball's soft cap system. Under that system, a progressive "luxury tax" is paid by a team when its player payroll exceeds the league's annual maximum. That limit is set each season. For 2013, the cap was set at $178 million. This amount is, in fact, far beyond the revenue-generating capacity of nearly all the teams in MLB—in 2013, not even half (14) of the 30 teams had a payroll above $100 million. The setting of the luxury tax limit at $178 million is testament to the negotiating skills of the players association and to the high level of influence possessed by a few powerful franchise owners. For the 2013 season, only the Yankees and the Los Angeles Dodgers had payrolls greater than $178 million. Since the tax has been put in place, the New York Yankees have paid nearly all of it. But those payments represent only a fraction of the revenues available to the Yankees. The club's exceptional revenue-generating capacity (over $470 million annually) allows it to compete aggressively in the free agent market each off-season. The Yankees are therefore in a position to include luxury tax payments in their spending budgets for each season, if they choose to do so.

However, since the luxury tax rate paid increases every year, it is widely believed that the Yankees will make an effort to bring their payroll below the luxury tax limit for at least a year or two. The Yankees reportedly paid a little over $29 million in luxury tax in 2013, a tax rate of 50 per cent based on a $236 million payroll, or $58 million over the limit. In 2014, the luxury tax limit will be increased to $189 million. If the Yankees manage to bring their payroll below this amount even for just one year, they will get a "clean slate" under the existing luxury tax rules. This cleaning of the slate in 2014 would mean that the next time the club brings its payroll over the limit (most likely in 2015, given their cash flow), it will only have to pay the luxury tax rate of a first-time offender—17 per cent. Reducing the luxury tax rate from 50 per cent to 17 per cent would save the Yankees millions of dollars. A luxury tax rate of 17 per cent in 2013, for example, would have reduced the team's annual luxury tax bill by $16 million—enough to sign a very good player!

The absence of a hard salary cap as a share of expected revenues in MLB has led to enormous differences in team payrolls, allowing historical trends to continue and severely limiting the ability of a team with a low payroll to compete on the field on a regular basis with the league's big spenders. True, through brilliant draft picks and clever management of personnel, a team can develop up-and-coming young stars and become a contender. The Tampa Bay Rays are a clear example of that practice, having made it to the World Series in 2008 and securing playoff spots in 2010, 2011, and 2013. Over this six-year span, the Rays maintained an average payroll of $55 million per season, about a quarter of the average annual New York Yankees payroll over the same period. Another great example is the Oakland Athletics. While their last World Series Championship was 24 years ago (1989), the A's have made the playoffs in six of the last fourteen years, including the last two (2012 and 2013), all the while fielding one of the lowest payrolls in MLB.

However, teams like the Rays and A's are always under pressure to increase their payrolls tremendously in order to keep the young stars that have made their team successful. These young players eventually become eligible for free agency, at which point they are likely to be lost to the New York Yankees, Boston Red Sox, or other teams with much deeper pockets. If Oakland and Tampa Bay do not increase their payrolls significantly, their only hope is to keep hitting home runs in the draft by identifying exceptional young players that the other teams miss. Clearly, over the longer term, a strategy of acquiring the best proven free agent talent available will beat out a strategy that depends on smart drafting and clever management of personnel.

But simply outspending other teams does not guarantee success, at least not on a regular basis. (See Table 6.) The Oakland A's, Pittsburgh Pirates, and Tampa Bay Rays were all part of the 2013 playoffs, even with the 26th, 27th and 28th highest payrolls, respectively. Conversely, the Chicago Cubs (who last won the World Series in 1908) and New York Mets (who last won in 1986) definitely provide evidence that money does not buy success every year. While both of these teams are now looking like "middle of the pack" spenders, they once carried some of the highest payrolls in baseball with very little to show for it. However, their deep pockets give these teams the ability to bounce back into contention rapidly by buying top talent on the free agent market—an advantage enjoyed by only a few teams.

Table 6
Major League Baseball Payrolls, 2013 Season and Win Rankings

Team	2013 payroll	2013 win ranking
New York (Yankees)	$228,995,945	12
Los Angeles (Dodgers)	$216,302,909	3
Philadelphia	$159,578,214	20
Boston	$158,967,286	1
Detroit	$149,046,844	5
San Francisco	$142,180,333	23
Los Angeles (Angels)	$142,165,250	17
Texas	$127,197,575	9
Chicago (White Sox)	$124,065,277	28
Toronto	$118,244,039	18
St. Louis	$116,702,085	4
Washington	$112,431,770	15
Cincinnati	$110,565,728	8
Chicago (Cubs)	$104,150,726	27
Baltimore	$91,793,333	11
Milwaukee	$91,003,366	26
Arizona	$90,158,500	16
Atlanta	$89,288,193	2
New York (Mets)	$88,877,033	24
Seattle	$84,295,952	22
Cleveland	$82,517,300	13
Kansas City	$80,491,725	14
Minnesota	$75,562,500	25
Colorado	$75,449,071	19
San Diego	$71,689,900	21
Oakland	$68,577,000	6
Pittsburgh	$66,289,524	7
Tampa Bay	$57,030,272	10
Miami	$39,621,900	29
Houston	$24,328,538	30

Sources: ESPN; National Hockey League.

For Canadian baseball fans, the reality of life in a non-binding salary cap world is that the country's only MLB team has generally had to rely on superior management capacity and talent selection—not on payroll—just to hope to make the playoffs, let alone win another World Series.[1] For the 2013 season, the ownership of the Blue Jays decided to "go out and shop" during the free agency signing season. In doing so, the Blue Jays lifted their payroll to over $118 million (10th highest in Major League Baseball) from $92 million for the 2012 season (17th highest). Hopes were high for the Blue Jays entering the 2013 campaign, but the Jays face another major challenge year after year—they play in the same division as the two of the richest teams in baseball (the Yankees and the Red Sox) and one of the few small-market teams (Tampa Bay) that is able to win consistently. As it turned out, the payroll bet taken by Toronto's ownership in 2013 did not pay off. The Blue Jays finished last in their division and posted only the 18th best record in baseball. But in baseball, hope springs eternal … and there is always next year.

Revenue Sharing

If a league is truly interested in creating a level playing field among its franchises, one of the fundamental steps it can take is to share a significant portion of revenue among the teams.

The NFL has set the standard when it comes to revenue sharing. During the early 1960s, Wellington Mara and his brother, Jack, owned the New York Giants and thereby controlled the NFL's largest market. But they agreed on a plan to share television revenue on a league-wide basis. That meant that the money generated from TV rights in the larger cities, such as New York, flowed equally to small-market teams, such as the Green Bay Packers. Perhaps because the money involved at that time was small, the richest NFL owners accepted the principle of revenue sharing—a key factor that has allowed the NFL to grow and prosper ever since.

---

1   When the Blue Jays won the World Series in 1992 and 1993, the franchise was among the highest spenders on player salaries. That allowed the Jays to attract late-career stars like Dave Winfield and Jack Morris to the team, while retaining exciting new talent, such as future Hall of Famer Roberto Alomar.

Today, the NFL and its franchises share more than 80 per cent of league and club revenues. TV broadcast revenues are shared equally among the franchises, as are merchandising revenues. For 2014–22, total TV contract revenues will jump to $40 billion, or nearly $5 billion annually. Even gate revenues are shared between the home and visiting teams, with 40 per cent of the ticket revenues for each game going to the visiting team (and the remaining 60 per cent going to the home team). NFL franchises recognize that they have a shared interest in maximizing total revenue. The league has prospered under these "all for one and one for all" arrangements. The end result: a highly competitive league with high and rising franchise values. There are now 20 NFL franchises (out of 32) that are worth $1 billion or more. This compares with but three Major League Baseball franchises (the New York Yankees, the Los Angeles Dodgers, and the Boston Red Sox) and five soccer teams (Manchester United, Real Madrid, Barcelona, Arsenal, and Bayern Munich).

Overall, the NHL's revenue-sharing and subsidy system is messy and creates conditions for divisiveness among franchises.

Now compare the NFL approach to the NHL's revenue-sharing system. To start, national TV revenues for the NHL are low compared with what the other leagues get from their TV contracts. For years, expansion of the NHL across the United States took place with one goal in mind—to sell hockey south of the Canadian border. At stake, potential huge television contracts with one or more major broadcasters. The NHL does have a national TV contract in the United States, but the revenue it brings in is nothing close to what football and baseball do. The NHL's new contract with NBC has boosted the league's U.S. national TV revenues to $200 million annually—up from $75 million in 2011–12.

In Canada, the CBC pays the NHL about $100 million in broadcast fees annually, and TSN reportedly pays about $40 million a year. The new TV deal with Rogers will increase revenues significantly. Nevertheless, even with total national TV revenues rising to about

US$600 million a year, much of the revenue shared among the NHL teams comes directly out of the wealthier teams' pockets—a key difference.

The NHL's complex revenue-sharing system is part of the collective bargaining agreement reached with the players. The revenue-sharing system was completely revamped under the 2013 agreement—and it is complicated. In a nutshell, the revenue-sharing pot has revenues from three sources. The first, accounting for 50 per cent of the pot, is contributions from the top-ten teams in terms of gross revenues. The second is gate receipts from home playoff games, of which 35 per cent goes to the pot. And the third source is general league revenues.[2] These funds are to be divided up among recipient teams to help bring them up to a "targeted team player compensation" level, which is a calculated value somewhere between the annual salary floor and the salary band mid-point, based on a number of factors. Teams receiving revenue-sharing funds are also supposed to submit business plans to the league on how to improve their operations and financial performance, and they can receive loans or grants to help in that regard from the new "Industry Growth Fund." Got it?

The new NHL revenue-sharing system is complicated, but it is guided by the answer to a fundamental question: Why would the NHL provide subsidies to its weaker franchises? Protecting the current and future value of the stronger franchises is the principal reason. The bankruptcy of any franchise is not a good signal to send to prospective investors in other NHL franchises, and simply moving franchises between cities means there are no franchise expansion fees to share. (While the deal to move the Atlanta Thrashers to Winnipeg did include a $60-million relocation fee, that amount is far less than what the league would receive from the owners of a new franchise. Only when the ongoing costs of subsidizing a struggling franchise become uncomfortably large does the relocation of a weak franchise become an attractive idea to the other franchise owners.) A secondary reason for the NHL to provide subsidies to weaker franchises is to maintain its profile in prime television markets—a key to winning larger U.S. national TV contracts in future.

2   Dirk Hoag, "The 2013 NHL CBA: New Revenue Sharing Program Could Help the Nashville Predators," *On the Forecheck*, June 7, 12013.

Overall, the NHL's new revenue-sharing and subsidy system is complex. It also clearly distinguishes the top-ten grossing franchises from the others and gives them an explicit role in transferring revenues to financially weaker franchises. The system needs to be tested in action—but if it works, the NHL may experience a period of relative stability such as it has not seen for a decade.

Access to Player Talent

All the major pro sports leagues have now adopted the same operating model for player talent—an entry draft and free agency at some point in a player's tenure with the league. The specific details of the entry draft and free agency, however, vary considerably among the leagues.

Expanding the pro sports talent pool has been key to maintaining a high standard of play at a time of steady expansion in all the North American leagues in recent decades.

In the case of the NHL, the league introduced its amateur entry draft in 1963 to give all teams a relatively equal chance to sign young talent.[3] Today, players who will be at least 18 years old on September 15, but will be no older than 20 on December 31 (or 21 for non-North American players), are eligible for selection in the June draft. The draft order is based on where the teams finished during the past season, with the lowest-placed teams picking first. (However, there is also a lottery designed to discourage those teams from deliberately weakening their rosters in the final weeks of a season in order to improve their draft position.)

Globalization has also become a factor of growing importance in pro sports that have international appeal. Forty years ago, more than 90 per cent of the players in the NHL were Canadian. Today, that share

---

3   Sam Pollock, the general manager of the Montreal Canadiens in the 1960s and 1970s, demonstrated that the best young players (such as Guy Lafleur) could still be selected by the top teams through skilful use of trades to secure draft picks.

has fallen to about 50 per cent. The U.S. share of the NHL talent pool has grown to about 20 per cent, and Europeans now account for about 30 per cent (although this share is being challenged by the three-year-old Kontinental Hockey League in Russia). Baseball first looked to the Caribbean and Latin America to expand its existing American player base, and has more recently spread its talent search to the Asia-Pacific region and Canada. The NBA has the most diversified talent pool. It draws players from around the globe. More than 30 countries are represented in the NBA, with foreign-born players accounting for about 20 per cent of NBA rosters. Expanding the pro sports talent pool has been key to maintaining a high standard of play at a time of steady expansion in all the North American leagues in recent decades. At the same time, international expansion of the talent pool has helped to grow the popularity of these sports in international markets.

Changes in Competitive Conditions

On occasion, a league will recognize that a franchise, or group of franchises, is facing particular challenges and will take special steps to make the financial and competitive playing field more level. A decade ago, for example, the NHL agreed to help struggling Canadian franchises that had been battered by the effects of a weak Canadian dollar. (Today, the Canadian dollar is trading at much closer to par with the U.S. greenback, which radically changes the circumstances of Canadian teams playing in North American sports leagues.)

And as discussed earlier, the NHL today provides operating subsidies for teams in smaller markets that are struggling with low attendance. The NHL thus appears to face chronic challenges with respect to competitive conditions among its franchises.

Conclusion

Whether a league implements a level playing field among its franchises, and how it does so, says a great deal about its business philosophy and the distribution of economic power within the league. The business model of the NFL and its franchises, which share more than 80 per cent of league and club revenues, is vastly different from that of Major League Baseball, whose operating rules allow a few high-revenue teams to try to buy championships year after year. A level playing field—financially and in the win-loss column—is, therefore, far more likely in the NFL than it ever will be for Major League Baseball.

Not surprisingly, the level playing field concept is applied mostly to issues that directly affect the players—issues such as the creation of a hard or soft salary cap, the establishing of comparable access to player talent through a league entry draft, or the drawing up of free agency rights and rules.

> Whether a league implements a level playing field among its franchises, and how it does so, says a great deal about its business philosophy and the distribution of economic power within the league.

The NHL and NBA fall somewhere between the NFL and Major League Baseball in establishing a level playing field among franchises. The NHL has a player entry draft, salary cap, and free agency, but only limited direct revenue sharing among franchises. The NHL has compensated for the absence of aggressive revenue sharing by introducing targeted subsidy schemes when and where required. These selective schemes help to ensure that franchises survive as long as possible in a specific location, and thus do not drag down franchise values elsewhere or eliminate the potential value of shared expansion fees. Among the four major North American leagues, MLB makes the least effort to create a level playing field.

The NHL faces the most chronic challenges, in terms of keeping its weaker franchises afloat. A decade ago, the NHL was struggling to deal with the structural issue of a weak exchange rate for Canadian teams. The loonie is now a strong currency, but other challenges have emerged. There continue to be a number of weak franchises in the U.S.—particularly in southern markets, where there is no tradition of passion for hockey.

Under the latest collective bargaining agreement reached with the players in 2013, the top-ten grossing franchises have accepted an explicit role in transferring revenues to financially weaker franchises. The new system needs to be tested in action. Maybe the reduced salary cap and new revenue-sharing system will be sufficient to keep these franchises afloat; and maybe it won't be enough. The other franchise owners could eventually tire of propping up the weakest organizations and allow them to be moved to cities that truly value NHL hockey. We've already seen this happen with the move of the Atlanta Thrashers to Winnipeg. Others could follow.

Chapter 7
The Case of the Winnipeg Jets and the Quebec Nordiques

Some people are saying it is time to bring even more NHL hockey back to Canada! In this chapter, we look at the four market pillars of success—and how they apply to the loss of the Nordiques and the Jets in the mid-1990s. The Jets are back now. Could the Nordiques return as well?

In the mid-1990s, battered by a weak Canadian dollar and struggling to compete financially with bigger-market teams, two Canadian NHL franchises packed up and headed south. In Chapter 2, we argued that the success of a professional sports organization in any given market relies on four pillars of support. They are market size, income levels, a strong corporate presence, and a level playing field.

In this chapter, we put our four market pillars to the test by analyzing the departure of two Canadian-based National Hockey League franchises in the mid-1990s—the Quebec Nordiques and the Winnipeg Jets—as concrete examples. Were the departures of these two teams from Canada in the mid-1990s the result of weakness in these pillars? The Winnipeg Jets have returned, which raises these questions: Have things changed enough to allow the "new" Winnipeg Jets to be a long-term success in the NHL? And could the Quebec Nordiques return as well?

The Departures of the Winnipeg Jets and Quebec Nordiques

The Winnipeg Jets and Quebec Nordiques were both based in smaller cities, and both enjoyed passionate fan bases. Although neither team was able to bring home hockey's ultimate prize—the Stanley Cup— they were much beloved by their communities. In 1995, the Quebec Nordiques left for Denver, Colorado. The Winnipeg Jets moved to Phoenix, Arizona, the following year. A lot of tears flowed when the franchises packed up and left town. Clearly, the decision to leave could not be blamed on any lack of fan passion. So what exactly did happen? Let's look at the state of the four market pillars at that time.

Market Size

In Chapter 2, we hypothesized and estimated that the fan base required to support an NHL franchise is about 800,000. Interestingly, in the mid-1990s, the populations of both the Québec City and Winnipeg census metropolitan areas (CMAs) were below that threshold. Both stood at around 685,000. Moreover, Winnipeg was (and still is) home to a Canadian Football League (CFL) team, which required a market size of its own of at least 250,000. So in both cases, but particularly in the case of Winnipeg, the markets were being squeezed by the lack of a sufficiently large population base.

> Although neither team was able to bring home hockey's ultimate prize—the Stanley Cup—they were much beloved by their communities.

In fact, the Winnipeg market was facing saturation in terms of pro sports franchises. That's because the fan base required for each franchise is at least partly additive. While some fans will buy tickets to see more than one team, some won't, and others will divide their sports entertainment budgets between the teams. Let's consider a simple numerical example. A family devotes $1,000 per year to recreational activities, such as restaurant meals, movies, hockey games, football games, etc. If a family spends $350 to go to watch an NHL game, it will only have $650 left for the rest of the year. Will the family be able to afford to go to a CFL game in that same year? That would cost the family about $250, leaving only $400 for all other recreational activities in the year.

This simple example demonstrates why we believe the fan base requirement for additional professional sport franchises is at least partly additive. Some families will have the budget to attend games for multiple teams, but some others won't. In the case of Winnipeg, this principle means that the population required to support sustainable CFL and NHL franchises could well be as high as 1 million (since a population of 800,000 is needed for a successful NHL franchise and 250,000 for a CFL franchise). With a population of 685,000 in the mid-1990s, the Winnipeg area fell well below this threshold.

Income Levels

Our second pillar, the per capita income level of the market, was not an issue in the case of either Winnipeg or Québec City. As shown in Chapter 2, Winnipeg posted the sixth-highest level of per capita disposable income among Canada's nine largest cities in 1995. At that time, Winnipeg was ahead of Edmonton (seventh), Québec City (eighth), and Montréal (ninth). Moreover, Québec City had a higher level of per capita disposable income than Montréal. That suggests that income levels were not a factor in the Jets or the Nordiques leaving.

Corporate Presence

Our third pillar, a sound corporate presence, may have come into play, particularly for the Québec City market. There is no definite minimum number of corporations required in a community for a professional sports franchise to be viable. But in 2012, only 14 of Canada's 800 largest corporations were headquartered in Québec City, while

Winnipeg was home to 26. Are those numbers too low? Well, they are certainly a far cry from the 253 corporations headquartered in Toronto, 135 in Calgary, 97 in Montréal, and 94 in Vancouver. However, Winnipeg has more corporate headquarters than Edmonton (22) and Ottawa (18), both of which were home to NHL franchises in the mid-1990s and these franchises did not move. Based on the evidence, it is difficult to conclude that a relatively low corporate presence was (or is today) an issue for the Québec City or Winnipeg markets.

A Level Playing Field

The variable that played the biggest role in the departures of the Nordiques and the Jets in the mid-1990s was our fourth pillar—a level playing field. In particular, the Winnipeg Jets and Quebec Nordiques had to contend with a combination of higher income tax rates than U.S.-based teams and a plummeting Canadian dollar.

In 1979, when the Winnipeg Jets and Quebec Nordiques entered the NHL (moving over from the defunct World Hockey Association, or WHA), the average player salary was around US$100,000. When the teams left their Canadian homes in the mid-1990s, the average player salary had reached US$750,000. That works out to a 750 per cent rise in about 15 years, or a 55 per cent increase per year, compounded. Also adding to the problem is the fact that a player on a Canadian-based team pays a marginal income tax rate that is at least 10 percentage points higher than that of a player for a team located in the United States. Using this "10 per cent" rule of thumb, the average player on a Canadian-based team in 1979 was paying about US$10,000 in additional taxes by playing in Canada. By the mid-1990s, that same player was pulling in something like $75,000 less in after-tax income by playing in Canada. And those numbers were for the average player. A player making $3 million a year was losing US$300,000 in after-tax income if he was playing for a Canadian-based team. By the mid-1990s, this tax gap had become a serious challenge for Canadian NHL franchises as they struggled to attract and retain player talent—and this was particularly true for the two smallest market franchises.

On top of the tax-related challenge, the exchange rate between the Canadian and U.S. dollars was becoming an increasingly important factor. From 1979 (when the Jets and the Nordiques entered the NHL) to the mid-1990s, the Canadian dollar progressively depreciated vis-à-vis its U.S. counterpart. In 1979, the Canadian dollar was worth more than 85 cents U.S. By the mid-1990s, it had declined to around 70 cents. This depreciation had a strong impact on the financial health of Canadian NHL franchises, which generate revenues in Canadian dollars but have to remain competitive with teams generating revenues in U.S. dollars. While not all NHL players were paid in U.S. dollars in the mid-1990s (unlike today), players' contract negotiations were still based on what players of "equal talent" playing for U.S.-based teams were getting in terms of spending power.[1]

The Winnipeg Jets and Quebec Nordiques had to contend with a combination of higher income tax rates than U.S.-based teams and a plummeting Canadian dollar.

To illustrate the impact of the exchange rate on team finances, consider the following example. In the mid-1990s, the Quebec Nordiques and Winnipeg Jets were carrying payrolls of about US$20 million. In Canadian dollar terms, this would have meant a payroll of C$23.5 million if the 1979 exchange rate had still been in effect. Instead, the actual cost was about C$28.5 million. By the time the franchises were deciding to move to the United States, the depreciation of the Canadian dollar alone was costing the Nordiques and the Jets about C$5 million a year. If we assume the average price of a ticket was about C$50 at the time, both teams needed to sell 100,000 more tickets over a season to absorb the impact of the exchange rate. That is equivalent to increasing the average attendance by more than 2,000 people per game—a pretty tall order, particularly for the two franchises based in the Canada's smallest NHL markets,

1   Thanks to former NHL player Jim Kyte for this insight.

and with two of the smaller rinks in the league. Even if rink capacity had not been an issue, getting that many extra people into the stands every single night would be an extremely demanding feat.

The exchange rate continued to depreciate and the negative impact of the income tax rate differential grew as salaries rose. The business conditions became increasingly difficult for most Canadian teams and players became less enthusiastic about playing for a team based in Canada. While the other Canadian teams did not fold despite facing the same set of circumstances, they struggled financially. And the Nordiques and Jets were particularly squeezed by the smaller size of their markets, and by the relatively weak corporate presence in their cities. The final decision to move both these franchises south to U.S. cities was a rational business response to the deteriorating overall market conditions.

That was then, but what about today? Has the situation changed enough so that the reborn Winnipeg Jets will be successful over the long term? Can Québec City now support an NHL franchise? Once again, a look at our four market pillars helps provide an answer to these questions.

Market Size

As noted earlier, Québec City and (particularly) Winnipeg were stretched markets for the NHL back in the mid-1990s. Much has changed since then. Both CMAs have posted robust population growth since the mid-1990s. By 2012, the Québec City and Winnipeg CMAs both had populations over 770,000—more than 12 per cent above the 685,000 levels of the mid-1990s. Since we believe that a market size of 800,000 is needed to support a successful NHL franchise, both markets are clearly in a much better position to do so than they were 15 years ago. Both remain small markets, but both are at least very close to the 800,000 threshold.

Income Levels

There is also good news for Québec City and Winnipeg when it comes to our second pillar, per capita income. Income levels have grown significantly in both cities since the mid-1990s. Winnipeg's per capita income level grew by 2.8 per cent per year between 1995 and 2012, while per capita income grew 3 per cent per year in Québec City over the same time frame. Winnipeg's income level was above that of Montréal in 2012. In the case of Québec City, the per capita income ranking has improved since the Nordiques moved to Denver, going from eighth out of Canada's nine largest urban centres to seventh place over that time.

> The biggest change in favour of the reborn Winnipeg Jets and the potential return of an NHL franchise in Québec City is the evolution of our fourth pillar—the level playing field.

Given that the NHL operates in both Canada and the United States, and that the NHL is free to choose cities in either country when it considers new markets, should we be comparing Winnipeg's and Québec City's income levels with those of U.S. cities as well? Perhaps, but our point here is that the income levels of Québec City and Winnipeg are in line with other Canadian cities that are currently home to financially stable NHL teams.

Corporate Presence

Our analysis concerning our third pillar—corporate presence—was provided in Chapter 2 using 2012 data, which means that it reflects today's reality. Neither Winnipeg nor Québec City can compete with Toronto, Calgary, Montréal, or Vancouver when it comes to their number of corporate head offices. And it could be argued that this pillar is even more important now than it was in the mid-1990s, since growth in ticket prices has generally outpaced growth in per capita income. Thus, professional sports teams need corporations to buy boxes even more today.[2] Therefore, it will be critical for the Jets organization to maintain and nurture its partnership with Winnipeg-area corporations. Our advice to any group hoping to bring a franchise to Québec City: ensure that corporations based there are on board prior to securing a franchise, rather than waiting until after a franchise is secured before lining up corporate support in the form of box and season ticket sales and advertising.

A Level Playing Field

The biggest change in favour of the reborn Jets and a potential return of an NHL franchise to Québec City is the evolution of our fourth pillar—the level playing field. Two significant changes have occurred that have levelled the playing field considerably:

- The Canadian dollar is now hovering around 90 cents U.S.—far above where it was a decade earlier.
- A player salary cap has been established.

We mentioned the significant costs that NHL teams in Canada were forced to bear due to the depreciation of the Canadian dollar. When the Nordiques and the Jets entered the NHL, the dollar was worth 85 cents (U.S.). By the time they moved south of the border in the mid-90s, the dollar had fallen to around 70 cents (and it would continue falling until bottoming out around 62 cents in early 2002). But this depreciation has been more than reversed.[3]

The rebound of the loonie drastically improves the playing field for all Canadian NHL franchises—and indeed all pro sports franchises in Canada that have significant portions of their operating costs denominated in U.S. dollars. These franchises no longer have to find an extra 20, 30, or even 40 per cent in revenues in Canadian dollars, compared with their U.S.-based counterparts, in order to pay player salaries denominated in U.S. dollars. Canadian teams are now able

---

2   Of course, if a professional sports team wants corporations to get involved, the team will need a facility that contains sufficiently attractive corporate boxes. This was lacking in the buildings used by the Winnipeg Jets and Quebec Nordiques in the mid-1990s.

3   The rapid rise of emerging markets—such as China and India—will sustain demand for Canada's commodities, which, in turn, will support a strong Canadian dollar for years to come.

to pay their players their market value without a large exchange rate premium, which is a huge gain, although the income tax differential remains and works against Canadian teams.

Last but not least, the NHL has made an effort (in contrast to Major League Baseball) to ensure that teams located in smaller markets are able to compete. It did so by introducing a salary cap, and a revised revenue-sharing system.[4] While we recognize that the NHL salary cap might not be perfect and that the new revenue-sharing system is still untested, the NHL has gone a long way to helping its smaller-market franchises. Under these conditions, the "new" Winnipeg Jets and a potential new franchise in Québec City could compete with larger markets on an ongoing basis.

> While the NHL salary cap might not be perfect and the league could do more when it comes to revenue sharing, the NHL has gone a long way to helping its smaller-market franchises.

The Winnipeg market, however, still faces a potential obstacle to its long-term success—pro sports saturation. Winnipeg is home (again) to both a CFL and an NHL franchise and maintaining the financial health of both franchises could be challenging over the long haul. Winnipeg's population did grow by over 12 per cent since 1995, bringing it to a little over 780,000. In addition to the NHL Jets, the city is home to a long-time CFL franchise—the Blue Bombers. According to our analysis, a CFL franchise requires a potential fan base of at least 250,000. And for both a CFL and an NHL franchise to be successful in the same market, we estimate the required population of that market at as high as 1 million. There may be other circumstances that will

---

4   The NHL salary cap also comes with a salary floor, which was set at US$44 million for the 2013–14 season—more than double the payrolls that Quebec and Winnipeg were carrying at the time of their departure in the mid-1990s.

allow Winnipeg to host both a CFL and NHL franchise successfully, such as exceptional passion among the fan base, but the basic market condition of population size indicates that there could be challenges ahead.

Our concern here is not the short term. The Jets sold out for the first three seasons in a matter of minutes back in the fall of 2011. The return of the Jets obviously created an enthusiasm that ensured the team success for a number of years to come. For their part, the Bombers finally have a new stadium, which inevitably provides a team with a positive "halo effect" with the fan base that want to see games at the new stadium. The concern we are raising here regarding pro sport market saturation is about the longer term—and only time will tell.

Conclusion

A look at our four market pillars helps to explain why the Quebec Nordiques and Winnipeg Jets had to leave Canada in the mid-1990s. In both these markets, however, things have improved since then. Their populations are higher, per capita disposable income has increased, the dollar is relatively strong, and the NHL has established a player salary cap that gives smaller markets a chance to be more competitive. However, the corporate presence in both markets remains relatively low. This is particularly true for Québec City. Nonetheless, we believe that the reborn Winnipeg Jets and a potential NHL franchise in Québec City have the right market conditions for long-term financial sustainability—but not at any price.

Other factors will need to be carefully monitored before we can conclude that the Jets or a new NHL franchise in Québec City have the sufficient overall conditions for success. Both markets remain relatively small. Moreover, any franchise that is brought to Québec City must be in solid financial condition to start. Should the franchise be an existing team? Or would an expansion team be a better fit? The National Hockey League would probably prefer the latter since the expansion fee could be worth around $300 million, or $10 million per existing team. Lastly, ownership will be critical, as with all professional sport franchises. In the case of both Québec City and Winnipeg, a committed, caring, and deep-pocketed owner is a prerequisite for success in both of these markets.

In the meantime, Québec City is addressing another very important issue: the venue. In the fall of 2012, work began on a new facility that will meet the standards of the NHL. Winnipeg already has a relatively new arena that seats just over 15,000, well below the average for NHL facilities—raising the question of whether it could be expanded to include more boxes and up to 3,000 additional seats.

Winnipeg faces an additional challenge. Is the fan base strong enough to support financially successful NHL and CFL franchises over the long term? Maintaining strong attendance for both teams will be a critical part of avoiding any risk of pro sports market saturation.

In sum, our four market pillars indicate that Québec City and Winnipeg can support NHL teams. But both markets also face challenges related to their relative population size. Their future success as pro sports markets will require dedication and hard work from all stakeholders.

Chapter 8
The Future of Major League Baseball in Canada

It's been nearly a decade since the Expos left Montréal. And the Blue Jays haven't played in the post-season since 1993. But Canadian baseball fans still dream of better days ahead, including the return of the Expos. Unfortunately, there are few signs of that dream turning into reality any time soon.

In 2004, the Montreal Expos packed up and moved to Washington. Was the move necessary? Could the Expos one day come back to Montréal? And based on the Expos' experience, what does the future hold for the Toronto Blue Jays?

As listed in Chapter 2, there are four market pillars required for a professional team sport to be financially successful in a given market. They are:

- a large enough (and growing) population;
- a relatively wealthy population;
- a sound corporate presence;
- a level playing field.

The Departure of the Montreal Expos

Ah, nos amours. Andre Dawson, Tim Raines, "The Kid" (Gary Carter), "le Grand Orange" (Rusty Staub), Steve Rogers—just a few of our old heroes. Many Canadians, particularly in Quebec, can tell you exactly where they were on "Blue Monday"—October 19, 1981—when journeyman Dodger Rick Monday hit a solo home run in the ninth inning off Expos' ace Steve Rogers. That proved to be the winning run, as the Dodgers took the fifth and deciding game of the 1981 National League Championship series by a score of 2–1. The Expos missed the World Series by one run ... *one run.*

Today's generation of sports fans may think that Montréal is not a baseball city. But Montréal was at one time very much a baseball city. In the 1980s, Montréal was attracting more fans to the city's Olympic Stadium than the Atlanta Braves were attracting to their home stadium. We all know how successful the Braves have been as a franchise since the beginning of the 1990s. The Expos could have been just as successful, if only they had gotten a little help from the Canadian dollar. So let's get one thing straight—the love for the game was there. While the Expos eventually did leave, it wasn't because the fans didn't care. Neither was it because, as our market pillars show, the city couldn't support a Major League Baseball team.

Market Size

The Expos' problem was not the size of the team's market, just as market size is not an obstacle to MLB returning to the city in the future. The Montréal census metropolitan area is home to nearly 4 million people. In a previous chapter, we said the fan requirement for an MLB franchise is 2.5 million people. So even in a market that includes the National Hockey League's Canadiens (an NHL franchise requires a population base of 800,000) and the Canadian Football League's Alouettes (a CFL franchise requires a base of 250,000), the population is still large enough to support a major league ball club. In 2012, Montréal added Major League Soccer (MLS) to the mix. But while the market might be a little squeezed, there is still enough room for an MLB franchise to succeed—as there was before the Montreal Expos left town.

Seattle and Pro Sports Market Saturation

Local markets can get saturated with pro sports, and Seattle is a prime example of a saturated market. The West Coast U.S. city was mentioned early in 2013 during discussions on the potential move of the Phoenix Coyotes. However, Seattle is flirting with pro sports saturation—too many teams in one place.

In 2012, Seattle's metropolitan area boasted a population of around 3.5 million. It has an MLB team (fan requirement of 2.5 million based on our formula), a National Football League team (minimum required fan base of 700,000), and an MLS franchise.[1] Seattle was also home to the SuperSonics (a National Basketball Association franchise, with a fan requirement of 800,000) until 2008 when the team was moved to Oklahoma City. (The move, although precipitated by franchise ownership, was likely also a leading indicator that the pro sports market in Seattle was reaching the saturation point.)

The combined estimated fan base requirement for an MLB, NFL, and NBA team in one market would be 4,000,000—almost 15 per cent (or 500,000) greater than Seattle's population. Interestingly, the city's MLS franchise (the Sounders) came to town in 2009 only after the NBA team had left Seattle. These days, Seattle is frequently mentioned as a potential home to both new NBA and NHL franchises. But given the city's pro sports history and the level of market saturation that already exists, Seattle would be hard-pressed to support an NBA franchise in addition to its three existing teams. An NHL franchise would be even more of a stretch.

---

1   The seat estimate for MLS is still to be clearly defined as attendance for many franchises is well below stadium capacity.

Market Wealth

Our second pillar—the wealth of the market—is not an issue for Montréal either. Montréalers have an appetite for entertainment and the financial means to avail themselves of such offerings. In Chapter 2, we did show that Montréal's disposable income per capita is below that of other large urban centres in Canada. But that certainly doesn't mean that Montréalers are too poor to afford a night out at the Olympic Stadium (or, better still, at a new baseball-specific venue located downtown).

Corporate Presence

Our third pillar—a strong corporate presence—is not a factor in keeping MLB from returning to Montréal. The city was home to the headquarters of 97 of Canada's 800 largest corporations in 2012 (as noted in Chapter 2). That puts Montréal third in this category behind only Toronto and Calgary.

A Level Playing Field

The market variable that did play a role in the departure of the Expos is our fourth pillar—a level playing field. The Expos had one of the best teams in Major League Baseball in the late 1970s and early 1980s. Unfortunately, despite all the talent on its roster, the team made it to the post-season only once. Not only did the failure to make the playoffs deny the Expos the potential glory of winning a World Series, it also cost the franchise the much-needed additional revenues that come with a post-season run. (There were no "wild cards" prior to 1994. From 1994 to 2011,[2] eight teams—as opposed to just four—advanced to the post-season, including the top-finishing second-place team in each league. Under that system, the Expos would also have made it to the post-season in 1979, when they had the second-best record in the majors but trailed Pittsburgh in their division.)

---

2   In 2012, MLB added a second wild card spot in each league. Under the new format, the two wild card teams play each other in a single-game elimination contest to determine who will go on to play in the Division Series.

As the Canadian dollar started its descent in the late 1970s, the Montreal Expos' financial troubles began. As Table 7 shows, the Canadian dollar was at parity with its U.S. counterpart over much of the first decade of the Expos' existence. But then the dollar started to fall in the late 1970s, a trend that intensified in the early 1980s, with the currency reaching a low of US$0.72 in 1986.

Table 7
Expos' Key Variables

Season	Expos' average attendance	MLB average attendance	Difference	Expos' final divisional standing	Value of C$ vs. US$
1969	14,970	15,530	−559	6	0.929
1970	17,589	17,142	446	6	0.958
1971	15,938	17,824	−1,886	5	0.990
1972	14,643	16,592	−1,949	5	1.009
1973	15,393	17,156	−1,762	4	1.000
1974	12,582	17,467	−4,886	4	1.022
1975	11,213	17,079	−5,865	5	0.983
1976	7,984	17,140	−9,156	6	1.014
1977	17,701	19,620	−1,919	5	0.94
1978	17,617	20,686	−3,069	4	0.877
1979	25,953	21,788	4,164	2	0.854
1980	27,261	21,733	5,529	2	0.855
1981	28,418	19,257	9,161	2*	0.834
1982	28,621	22,127	6,494	3	0.811
1983	28,650	22,170	6,480	3	0.811
1984	19,834	21,380	−1,546	5	0.772
1985	18,549	22,934	−4,385	3	0.732
1986	13,938	22,977	−9,039	4	0.720
1987	22,844	25,447	−2,603	3	0.754

(continued ...)

Table 7 (cont'd)
Expos' Key Variables

Season	Expos' average attendance	MLB average attendance	Difference	Expos' final divisional standing	Value of C$ vs. US$
1988	18,255	25,205	−6,950	3	0.813
1989	22,019	26,053	−4,034	4	0.845
1990	16,952	25,197	−8,245	3	0.857
1991	11,540	25,408	−13,868	6	0.873
1992	20,607	24,806	−4,199	2	0.827
1993	20,265	32,561	−12,297	2	0.775
1994	22,390	32,341	−9,950	1	0.732
1995	18,189	24,911	−6,722	5	0.729
1996	19,959	26,789	−6,830	2	0.733
1997	18,489	28,118	−9,629	4	0.722
1998	11,295	29,650	−18,355	4	0.674
1999	9,540	29,388	−19,848	4	0.673
2000	11,435	30,620	−19,184	4	0.673
2001	7,935	30,634	−22,699	5	0.646
2002	10,031	28,510	−18,478	2	0.637
2003	12,662	28,072	−15,410	4	0.714
2004	9,241	31,021	−21,780	5	0.768

*In 1981, Major League Baseball was hit by a strike that lasted from June 12 to August 9. When play resumed, the owners decided it would be a split season, with the pre-strike division leaders automatically qualifying for post-season play and getting home field advantage for the first-ever divisional playoffs. The Expos finished third in their division in pre-strike play but finished first in post-strike play, earning the right to meet the Philadelphia Phillies in the divisional playoff series (which the Expos would win in five games).
Sources: Baseball Almanac; The Bank of Canada.

The steady decline in the Canadian dollar brought along a significant rise in costs for the team, with the bulk of the pain coming from players' salaries. In 1986, for example, the Expos' team payroll stood at roughly US$10 million. That worked out to nearly $14 million in Canadian dollars. And with most of the franchise's revenues in Canadian dollars, the Expos soon saw a steady erosion in their capacity to field a strong team. At the same time, MLB player salaries were starting to increase rapidly. So the combination of rising salaries and a declining Canadian dollar made it harder for the Expos to field a competitive team. And as the Expos started to slide in the standings, attendance began to decline in tandem. While Montréalers have always loved baseball, they loved it a lot more when the Expos were winning. From 1979 to 1983, the Expos ranked second or third in their six-team division every year and were drawing an average of more than 26,000 fans per game—beating the MLB average by about 5,000 fans per game. (See Table 1.) But as the economics of the exchange rate and rising player salaries got in the way, the team's performance on the field suffered. And as the team slipped in the standings, so too did attendance.

In the eight seasons that followed (1984 to 1991), the Expos struggled to cope with a soft Canadian dollar and a much higher tax burden than their U.S. counterparts. The best they were able to manage were some third-place finishes in their six-team division. In 1991, they finished dead last. Average attendance per game over this eight-year time frame was 18,000—a drop of 8,000 per game from the 1979–83 period. At the same time, the MLB average grew—rising to more than 24,000 per game. So the Expos, who had attracted 5,000 more fans per game than the MLB average from 1979 to 1983, were now attracting 6,000 fewer fans per game than the MLB average. By 1991, the Expos were averaging a dismal 11,540 in attendance, or almost 14,000 fewer paying fans than the MLB average.

In 1992, the Expos were on the upswing again. Between 1986 and 1991, the dollar had risen five cents to US$0.87, giving the Expos more financial capacity to attract talent and, more importantly, to retain the top young players they had acquired through some great drafting. In both 1992 and 1993, the Expos finished second in their division—and attendance rose back above 20,000 per game (though still well below the MLB average of 27,000 per game).

And then came a year of both glory and tragedy for the Expos. In 1994, the Expos were attracting over 20,000 fans per game for a third straight year. The franchise was full of potential, able to field a team that combined rising and experienced stars—players like Pedro Martinez, Larry Walker, Moises Alou, and Cliff Floyd—and managed by the legendary Felipe Alou. In August 1994, Montréal had the best record in baseball and was headed toward the playoffs. Many pundits were picking the Expos as early World Series favourites.

> In August 1994, Montréal was headed toward the playoffs. Then, on August 11, MLB players went on strike. After this, the trust between the Montréal fans and Major League Baseball was broken.

Then fate intervened. On August 11, MLB players went on strike. The strike wiped out the remainder of the 1994 season, including the post-season. Once again, the fans' hearts were broken—just as they had been in 1981 when the Expos were knocked out of the post-season by Rick Monday's home run. Even worse, the trust between the Montréal fans and Major League Baseball was broken.

When MLB returned the following spring, fans everywhere demonstrated their displeasure. Average attendance at MLB games dropped, going from more than 32,000 in 1994 to under 25,000 in 1995. Attendance at Expos games also fell. The Expos attracted an average of just 18,000 fans per game in 1995—and that was only the beginning of a long downward slide. Over the club's final seven seasons (1998 to 2004) in Montréal, the Expos' averaged barely 10,000 fans per game. Elsewhere, the fans eventually returned, with MLB as a whole attracting an average of over 30,000 per game by 2004—three times more than what the Expos managed that year. And to make matters worse, the Canadian dollar began to fall again in 1992, further aggravating the Expos' financial condition. (Add to that, questionable ownership and a disintegrating and unpopular venue … but we won't go there.)

With fan support dwindling and the dollar weakening, corporate appetite for sponsorship dried up. Ownership was suffering major financial losses, and it was only a matter of time before the team left town. Following the 2004 season, the franchise was moved to Washington, D.C., and renamed the "Nationals." The Expos' tri-coloured cap became a collector's item.

Could the Expos Return to Montréal? Could the Blue Jays Move South?

Should Montréal fans hold out hope that the team they once referred to as "nos amours" could one day return to their city? Even though the market pillars are in place for success in Montréal, we don't think the Expos will return any time soon. There is one major economic factor working against a return to Montréal—the lack of a level playing field among franchises. While the Canadian dollar might be stronger than a decade ago, it would be tough to find an individual or corporation willing to bring an MLB team back to Montréal knowing that the club would struggle to be competitive. A new franchise in Montréal could probably afford a payroll similar to that of the Tampa Bay Rays, Oakland A's, or Pittsburgh Pirates (which averaged about $65 million in 2013). That would leave the team in the bottom third of the payroll rankings—and likely to struggle to be competitive most seasons. It is wonderful for their fans that the Rays, A's, and Bucs made the playoffs in 2013, but that was due largely to exceptional management, which will have a hard time reproducing those results consistently against teams with much larger player payrolls.

Moreover, a new stadium would probably be needed to make baseball work again in Montréal. That would require a huge investment in a team with little near-term hope of success in the standings. One possibility would be to find an owner for whom the Expos would be only one part of a business empire containing media interests. (But even here, the Expos would likely be competing for attention with the possible return of an NHL team to Québec City.) Unless an owner with extremely deep pockets and a readiness to lose money shows up, we fear that baseball won't be returning to Canada's second-largest city any time soon.

What about Toronto? Is the city in any danger of losing the Blue Jays to relocation? We don't think so. The situation in Toronto is different from Montréal. The franchise can look forward to reasonably healthy revenues over the coming years, and a quality stadium is already in place. With the Canadian dollar relatively healthy and expected by The Conference Board of Canada to stay that way for some time to come, we believe Blue Jays fans can rest easy for the foreseeable future—at least from an economic standpoint. Moreover, there is significant cross-ownership linking the Blue Jays franchise, the stadium, and a cable broadcaster, which aligns and strengthens the revenue flow for all three entities. In fact, the Blue Jays showed off their financial bench strength prior to the 2013 season by boosting their player payroll by a significant $26 million—although, unfortunately for the Jays, they had little to show for it.

Montréal today has the necessary market conditions to be home to an MLB franchise, but the competitive conditions in the MLB make it non-appealing to most potential investors.

Because MLB does not have a hard salary cap (relying instead on various measures to transfer revenues to weaker franchises), the Blue Jays, even with their increased payroll, still can't compete with the powerhouse franchises when it comes to purchasing power. Superior management and talent selection will be the only way for the team to make the playoffs, let alone win another World Series. And as we noted earlier, Toronto has the added misfortune of playing in the same division as two of the richest teams in baseball—the New York Yankees and the Boston Red Sox. Even after increasing their 2013 payroll by a whopping 28 per cent, the Blue Jays finished last (again) in the American League East division. And while we don't want to be pessimists, with the playing field tilted significantly against their franchise, Blue Jay fans should not be surprised if their team's best hope in the coming years is to be in the running for a possible wild card spot.

Conclusion

Montréal today has the necessary market conditions in place to be home to an MLB franchise. The city is large and wealthy enough, has a healthy corporate presence, and the stronger Canadian dollar is a key factor in its favour. But among the major professional leagues, MLB has the least-level playing field—and that (along with the lack of a quality baseball facility) makes Montréal unappealing to most potential owners as a site for an MLB franchise. Still, we are not closing the door entirely to the possibility of MLB returning to the city. If a media conglomerate were to bring a team to Montréal, the synergy could work. With a regular season schedule of 162 games, a team in Montréal would provide great TV, radio, and Internet content. The number of sports specialty channels continues to rise, and along with them the demand for content. An MLB team in Montréal would be highly appealing for the right media group. Such a group could be a competitor to Rogers, which owns the Toronto Blue Jays.

The Blue Jays are a different case. While the team cannot hope to compete on payroll with the top-spending teams, the franchise does have healthy and stable revenues. The team also has a quality facility and makes money (most years) for its corporate owner. But, while Blue Jays fans would love to see their team in a post-season game in Toronto, the likelihood of that happening in the near future remains an open question.

Chapter 9

Some Real-World Examples of Why Pro Sports Franchises Succeed ... or Fail

Strong ownership and management, adequate playing facilities, and a commitment to building fan support are keys to success when it comes to pro sports franchises. And there is no shortage of examples that illustrate this fact.

For fans, professional sports entertainment is fundamentally about "their" team and its success on the playing field. But to remain consistently competitive, those teams must also succeed financially. Chapter 6 set out the key factors that help determine why some pro sports franchises succeed, everything else being equal, while others languish. These factors include:

- ownership and management strength;
- the availability of adequate playing facilities;
- fan support for the team.

Examples abound of how these three factors affect the health of pro sport franchises. Here are a few concrete cases.

Ownership and Management Strength

A key dimension of team success, both athletically and financially, is the strength of the ownership and management of the franchise. Ownership helps to establish the culture of the organization. Ownership selects the management team that, in turn, runs the franchise as a business and oversees the team on the field or rink.

For every positive example of sustained ownership and management strength that has resulted in sustained competitive and financial success (such as the National Hockey League's Detroit Red Wings after Mike Ilitch bought the team in 1982), there are examples of teams that have suffered a chronic failure at the ownership and/or management level. The Phoenix Coyotes, the Florida Panthers, and the Atlanta Thrashers (who have since packed up and moved to Winnipeg) are examples of franchises where something important was (or is) missing at the level of ownership and/or management—problems that go beyond the four market pillars for success explored in Chapter 2 or the competitive conditions of the league discussed in Chapter 3.

Case 1: Management Matters—The Fumbling of the Ottawa Rough Riders

Over time, weak franchise management and poor decision-making can create a self-perpetuating downward cycle of mediocrity and steady decline that eventually leads to the failure of the franchise. The Ottawa Rough Riders stand as a clear example of combined ownership/management failure and how it can lead to a downward spiral.

The Ottawa Rough Riders were once the pride of Canada's national capital and its surrounding regions. Founded in 1876, the Canadian Football League team won nine Grey Cup championships, including four from 1968 to 1976. The Rough Riders were a model of a successful—and sustainable—sports franchise during that period. The team was owned by well-capitalized local business leaders and run frugally by managers who treated it as a business rather than a hobby. Although privately owned, the organization had deep community connections through its ownership and its most visible employees—

the players. The Rough Riders developed a loyal and passionate (albeit demanding and vocal) customer base. Their fans expected success, but also viewed the team as a source of personal pride.

For every positive example of sustained ownership and management success, there are examples of teams that have suffered a chronic failure at the ownership and/or management level.

In the late 1970s, the success started to run out. The descent was slow at first. The Rough Riders had their last winning season in 1979, appeared in their last Grey Cup final in 1981, and won their last playoff game in 1982. While many of the elements for on- and off-the-field success remained in place into the 1980s, looking back it is clear to see that changes in ownership and management during this period were turning points for the franchise. The franchise changed hands in 1977. And as the franchise began to sputter and then spiral downward, the Riders went through six more ownership changes, starting in 1987 and ending with the folding of the club in 1996.

Year after year of losing seasons led to coaching, management, and—ultimately—ownership changes. Each new owner left the franchise further behind its competitors. On the field, the Riders could not keep up with other CFL teams. And off the field, the franchise steadily lost customers to the increasing entertainment options available in the Ottawa market. Gimmicks, such as pre-game concerts and giveaways of tickets and paraphernalia, proved to be no substitute for fielding a competitive team.

In their final seasons, the Rough Riders went from being merely a bad team to being a public embarrassment. The franchise steadily eroded the one intangible that keeps sports fans coming back to cheer on their team—pride. A fan base that had for decades consistently responded to every hopeful sign finally lost interest.[1]

1   Thanks to Brent Dowdall, our colleague at The Conference Board of Canada and author of *Turnover: The Fumbling of the Ottawa Rough Riders* (Carp, Ont.: Baird O'Keefe Publishing, 1999), for providing this succinct assessment of the collapse of the Ottawa Rough Riders.

The lesson here for all sports franchises is that success is not preordained. It doesn't come by simply opening the stadium doors and appealing to fans' memories of past glories. Ownership must see its investment as a long-term commitment—at least 10 years into the future, not a one-to-five-year team rescue or a quick asset flip. Fans have to be treated as what they are—customers who have choices about where and how they spend their time and money. Finally, quality counts … a lot.

Case 2: Liverpool FC—How Ownership, Finances, and Performance Are Linked

Questionable financial decisions by owners and management can clearly affect a franchise's results on the field. The recent history of the English football club Liverpool provides a current example of how ownership, management, and team performance are interlinked. Liverpool FC was acquired in 2007 by two Americans—George Gillett and Tom Hicks—through a leveraged buy-out that relied heavily on debt financing. The new owners were speculating, with borrowed money, that franchise values for top-tier English Premiership football teams would continue to rise as they had during the 1990s and 2000s.

However, the 2008–09 financial crisis and recession, combined with poorer-than-expected results on the field, hurt club revenues. The negative spiral effect soon set in. As the owners became less willing to spend the millions required to acquire new top players, the team's results began to suffer. Liverpool FC supporters became increasingly unhappy with the club's absentee owners. Financial conditions and team performance declined in parallel. And as the team's success on the pitch faded in 2009 and 2010, the financial institutions that held debt in the franchise began to get nervous and pressed for repayment. But the U.S. owners were badly overstretched on many fronts, increasing the risk that the owners would be unable to repay the debt that was the financial underpinning for Liverpool FC. By the summer of 2010, the team was facing a growing financial and competitive crisis—and the passionate fan base was beginning to revolt, stalking the owners (literally) and threatening the banks that had provided the debt financing.

The situation was resolved in October 2010 through the sale of the club to another U.S. investor, Boston Red Sox owner John Henry. Fortunately for the franchise, the rescue came before the downward spiral could advance to the point of a critical competitive decline and financial collapse. The new owners quickly changed team management, sacking Roy Hodgson and bringing back a popular previous manager, Kenny Dalglish. After finishing in eighth position in the 2011–12 season, the worst league finish in 18 years, Dalglish was sacked. He was replaced by Brendan Rodgers, who guided the team to a seventh-place finish in the Premiership but with hopes for better results in 2013–14.

> Ownership must see its investment as a long-term commitment—at least 10 years into the future, not a one-to-five-year team rescue or a quick asset flip.

Better results on the pitch, combined with stronger ownership, are creating a positive spiral, lifting Liverpool's financial and competitive performances and increasing the club's capacity to buy additional top-quality talent. This positive change in ownership, financial strength, and management has helped propel Liverpool FC back into the top rungs of the British Premier League and European football once again in the 2013–14 season. And the Champions League beckons.

Pro Sports Facilities

If a team is to succeed financially, it must have a professional sports facility of appropriate scale and quality. A team's financial success can be derailed by a poor facility, no matter how great the market or how supportive the league conditions. At the same time, financial and competitive success can, in some cases, be restored by the construction of a new building.

Case 3: Montréal's Olympic Stadium vs. Cleveland's Jacobs/Progressive Field

How important is a good venue to the success of a baseball franchise? The lack of a baseball-specific stadium was not the sole factor behind the departure of the Montreal Expos in 2004. However, having to play within the concrete confines of Montréal's Olympic Stadium certainly did not help the team's cause. The "Big O" was not designed for baseball. The crowd was far from the field and sightlines were poor. The stadium was supposed to have a retractable, parachute-style roof, but it took over a decade after the Expos moved in for the roof to be added—and then it proved to be impractical to retract and was later replaced by a fixed roof. Given how short Montréal summers are, the thought of spending a sunny summer day indoors watching baseball did not appeal to fans—just as sitting in the open for baseball games on a cold April day before the roof was in place had not been an attractive idea. The stadium was also perceived as being too far from the city's downtown core—another strike against it. By the early 1990s, the stadium was showing acute signs of fatigue, and some fans began to fear for their safety after a 55-tonne concrete slab fell on to an exposed walkway in 1991.

While being forced to play in an aging or poorly designed facility can cripple a Major League Baseball franchise, a new facility can help revive it. Just ask the Cleveland Indians. For decades, the franchise was a laughing stock. The Indians played in Cleveland Municipal Stadium—a cavernous, multi-purpose stadium on the shores of Lake Erie that was nicknamed the "Mistake by the Lake." From 1960 to 1993, the Indians managed just one third-place finish and six fourth-place finishes. The rest of the time was spent at or near the bottom of the standings. That began to change in the early 1990s, as ownership made a concerted effort to rebuild the franchise—including the construction of a new $175-million downtown ballpark that was financed on a roughly 50-50 basis by private and public sector money. The Indians opened Jacobs Field (later renamed Progressive Field) in 1994. Attendance took off, and so did club revenues and the ability to spend on players. By August, the Indians were trailing their division by only one game—at which point the players strike wiped out the rest of the season.

> A team's financial success can be derailed by a poor facility, no matter how great the market or how supportive the league conditions.

The strike marked the beginning of a long slide to oblivion for the Expos. But when baseball returned in 1995, the Indians—playing in their new ballpark—continued to soar. Cleveland sprinted to a 100–44 record in 1995, winning its first ever divisional title. Cleveland then went on to a World Series berth for the first time since 1954. With tickets for every home game sold out before opening day, the Indians would repeat as AL Central champions in 1996—and they would do so again for three more years.

What a difference a quality facility can make! Baseball was a hit in Cleveland once again. No, it was not just due to the new downtown ballpark. And yes, there have been some losing seasons for the Indians in recent years. But the venue was a major part of the ownership's plan to turn the franchise around. And while the Expos did not pack up and move to Washington solely because they were stuck in the Big O, playing in an aging and non-baseball-friendly stadium certainly contributed to the team's problems.

Case 4: Replacing Le Colisée de Québec

While not as strikingly bad a venue as the Olympic Stadium, Le Colisée de Québec posed serious limitations on the Quebec Nordiques franchise. The arena was home to the National Hockey League club from 1979 to 1995. By the end, it no longer met the requirements of a competitive NHL franchise. At a little over 15,000, its seating capacity was low. But Le Colisée's biggest shortcoming was its low number of corporate boxes. With player salaries rising rapidly, NHL teams needed the additional revenues that corporate boxes provide— but you can't sell more boxes if you don't have them. (The Winnipeg

Arena—home to the first incarnation of the Winnipeg Jets—faced the same limitations.) An aging arena was not the sole reason why the Nordiques left town, but it was one of the key factors behind the problems the franchise faced.

Today, plans to bring the Nordiques back to Québec City include the construction of a brand new arena, which is well under way even without an NHL tenant. Any serious attempt to bring back the Expos must also include the construction of a new venue, ideally in downtown Montréal. The challenge for Québec City will be to reap the maximum socio-economic benefits for the community, since the facility is entirely financed with public money.

Fan Support

The third factor for franchise success is the evolving appeal of specific pro sports to the consumer. All professional sports leagues and franchises need to be aware of how demographic trends and consumer tastes are evolving in their markets.

For example, an aging population might be good news for professional baseball, since older fans may be more attracted to the slower pace of the game. On the other hand, it could be a concern for hockey if it turns out that older fans are less attracted by the fast and sometimes violent game. Or an aging population could be a positive challenge for professional hockey franchises that develop marketing strategies aimed at retaining or attracting older fans (and their greater disposable incomes). The same holds true when it comes to winning young fans. Professional sports teams must work hard to attract young people to the game, since these fans will make up the sport's future client base.

Another very important phenomenon that professional sports teams must understand and integrate in their business models is the globalization of the population. Some markets are home to a large influx of immigrants every year. Toronto, Vancouver, and Montréal account for a significant share of Canada's growing immigrant population, and professional sports franchises must adjust to this new reality. It's no surprise that MLS pro soccer has taken off in these cities with their rapidly growing foreign-born populations. In Toronto, over 40 per cent of the population today was born outside Canada. For many, soccer is *their* team sport.

> All professional sports leagues and franchises need to be aware of how demographic trends and consumer tastes are evolving in their markets.

While newcomers to Canada make up a rapidly growing part of the potential fan base, average incomes among recent immigrants lag behind those of other Canadians, which may constrain their purchasing power when it comes to pro sports. Still, ignoring the demographic reality today could hurt the financial viability of professional sports teams in the future.

No matter the origin or the age of a fan, and no matter the adequacy of the marketing campaign, the ultimate strategy for any professional sports team is to put a quality product on the field or rink. People love a winner, and putting together a competitive team will sustain and grow fan interest. An individual may not be a fan at first, but he or she will soon enjoy the atmosphere a winning team generates within a community—gathering with friends to watch important games and maybe even participating in a victory parade at the end of the season. Professional sports can bring people together, and winning sure helps do that.

Conclusion

Throughout this book, we have demonstrated that when the fundamental market and league conditions are right, a pro sports franchise can succeed in a given market. And as described in Chapter 4, strong ownership and management can make a good franchise great. Conversely, poor ownership and management can undermine a franchise despite strong market and league conditions— as we saw with the demise of the Ottawa Rough Riders and the struggles of Liverpool FC before new owners were brought in. A quality playing facility can also make a huge difference to a franchise's success. That lesson can be clearly seen in the diverging stories of the baseball facilities in Cleveland and Montréal and their contribution to the home teams' success or failure. Then there is the case of Le Colisée in Québec City and why a new facility was absolutely essential to any efforts to bring an NHL team back to the city.

Lastly, there is the link between fan support for a given team and the evolving demographics in a community—and how important it is to adapt the team's market positioning to those demographic realities.

Chapter 10
Why Are Toronto Teams Financial Successes, but Competitive Flops?

In pro sports, competitive and financial success tend to go together. A team that struggles on the field for an extended period of time is likely to struggle at the box office, as well. But that hasn't been the story in Canada's largest city.

In recent years, most of Toronto's pro sports franchises have been financial successes, but consistent underachievers on the ice or field of play. What's going on? Is there something special about Toronto that turns its sports franchises into balance-sheet dynasties but competitive underperformers?

Using the analytical framework developed throughout this book, we conclude that strong market fundamentals for pro sports in the greater Toronto region mean that many Toronto teams can succeed financially without having to succeed competitively. A team's competitive results are ultimately determined by the selection and performance of its players and coaches, which is the responsibility of the franchise owners and the management they hire to run the team. But the market fundamentals suggest that Toronto's teams don't have to win to be financially successful, unlike teams in many smaller Canadian markets, where winning is often a prerequisite for financial success.

The Context

In recent years, most Toronto teams have fallen well short of the mark in terms of competitive success. The Leafs last won the Stanley Cup in 1967 and haven't made it back to the National Hockey League finals since. Just making the playoffs in the 2012–13 season was hailed as a triumph by the denizens of Leaf Nation (at least until the Leafs blew a 4–1 lead in the third period in game seven of their first-round series and lost in overtime to the Boston Bruins). Major League Baseball's Blue Jays won back-to-back World Series in 1992 and 1993, but have not made the playoffs since then. (Being stuck in baseball's toughest division doesn't help.) The Raptors have made the National Basketball Association playoffs three times in their 18-year existence but have advanced beyond the first round only once, a decade ago. Major League Soccer's Toronto FC just completed its seventh season and has never made it to the playoffs.

There are two successful exceptions to this dismal recent pattern. The Canadian Football League's Argonauts won the 2012 Grey Cup on their own field in Toronto, defeating the British Columbia Lions 35–22, and fielded a competitive team again in 2013. And the National Lacrosse League's Toronto Rock are arguably the model franchise in pro lacrosse—the club has won six NLL championships since 1999, most recently in 2011.

> The U.S. sports network ESPN rated Toronto as the worst city for professional sports in North America.

Still, despite the recent success of the Argos and the Rock, the common perception of Toronto today is that the city is not a pro sports powerhouse. In a 2010 column in *The Globe and Mail*, Jeffrey Simpson reached the conclusion that "Toronto indisputably remains the city of sports losers."[1] In June 2011, the U.S. sports network ESPN provided no less harsh a review when, in its survey of pro sports

1   Jeffrey Simpson, "When it Comes to Sports, Toronto Is a City of Losers," *The Globe and Mail*, April 10, 2010.

cities, it rated Toronto as the worst city for professional sports in North America. The ESPN survey ostensibly assessed how much a city's franchises in pro baseball, football, hockey, and basketball give back to the fans in exchange for the money and emotion the fans provide to their teams. The Leafs were ranked last among NHL franchises, and the Raptors were third-worst in the NBA. The Blue Jays scored the best ranking among Toronto teams—18th out of 30 MLB franchises.[2] (The Argonauts, Toronto FC, and the Rock were not included in the 2011 evaluation.)

The ESPN survey methodology is highly suspect. The survey relies on online voting by fans for a team or city—it is not random. And it measures fans' attitudes or perceptions, not the hard facts. It is more a popularity contest that an objective survey. Since it is conducted by a U.S. media firm, it may also have an implicit bias in favour of U.S.-based teams. And given the methodological weaknesses as well as the outcome, it is not surprising that members of Toronto's pro sports management cadre—including Leafs general manager at the time Brian Burke—flatly rejected the results.

But even if the ESPN survey isn't the most reliable source, it reflects the view that Toronto's pro sports teams are financial successes but competitive underperformers. Table 8 shows the profitability of some Toronto sports franchises (owned by major corporate entities), as estimated by Forbes. The Toronto Maple Leafs produce handsome profits that seemingly have little to do with the team's performance on the ice. The Blue Jays and Raptors also generated significant revenues in 2012, although the Jays showed a loss in 2012. Given the rise in their payroll in 2013, it will be interesting to see if the Forbes data will show yet another loss for the Blue Jays. Expert observers of the Toronto pro sports market suggest that net operating income for the Leafs may be even higher than the Forbes estimates (thanks to stronger overall revenues), and that of the Blue Jays lower (due to high player salaries). Unfortunately, there are no financial data publicly available for the Argonauts, Rock, or Toronto FC, which are privately held and are not covered by the Forbes survey. Still, we know that the Argos have had financially trying times

2   ESPN, "The Mag: Ultimate Standings 2011."

over the years, although owner David Braley is deeply committed to the success of the CFL. And we know that Toronto FC is owned by the same corporate entity that owns the Leafs and Raptors (Maple Leaf Sports and Entertainment, or MLSE, which in turn is owned by Bell and Rogers), has had very strong fan support at its games, and maintains firm control over its player payroll, so is likely to have positive financial results. And the Rock continues to be a cornerstone franchise for the NLL, which would not be possible if the team was continually bleeding red ink.

Table 8
Estimated Revenues and Operating Income, Selected Toronto Franchises, 2012
($ millions)

Franchise	Revenue	Operating income
Toronto Maple Leafs (NHL)	200	81.9
Toronto Raptors (NBA)	121	18.8
Toronto Blue Jays (MLB)	203	−4.8

Note: Toronto Maple Leafs' valuation as of November 2012, using numbers from the 2011–12 season; Raptors' valuation as of January 2013, using 2011–12 season revenues; Blue Jays' valuation as of March 2013, using 2012 season revenues.
Source: Forbes.

The Analysis

At the core of our analysis, once again, are our four market pillars for franchise success:

- population size;
- incomes;
- corporate presence;
- a level playing field.

The Market Pillars

Toronto's potential fan base is very large. The Greater Toronto Area (GTA) has a population of nearly 7 million when the census metropolitan areas of Toronto, Hamilton, and Oshawa are included. The population and employment base is also growing by more than

2 per cent annually and could approach 8 million by 2020 if the region's population grows as expected. The GTA fan base is hungry for sports entertainment, and there is unfulfilled demand for some pro sports (particularly hockey).

Toronto was fourth among Canadian cities in terms of per capita income—more than $30,000 in 2012. The large fan base, therefore, has the purchasing power necessary to support pro sports. In terms of head office presence, Toronto had 253 (or 31.6 per cent) of Canada's 800 largest corporate head offices in 2012. When these two factors are combined, it is clear that individuals and companies in the GTA have the requisite cash flow to purchase tickets, suites, advertising space, and merchandise for all of Toronto's pro sports franchises.

> Toronto's NHL, MLB, and NBA teams are now able to pay their players without a large exchange rate premium—a huge financial gain amounting to millions of dollars annually.

We called the fourth market pillar "a level playing field," which specifically means the exchange rate and tax rates in the market. The Canadian dollar is now trading closer to parity with its U.S. counterpart, and The Conference Board of Canada expects the loonie to remain in that range for the foreseeable future. The strengthening of the loonie levels the playing field for all Canadian pro sports franchises that have significant portions of their operating costs (notably, player salaries) denominated in U.S. dollars. Toronto's NHL, MLB, and NBA teams are now able to pay their players without a crippling added exchange rate premium—a huge financial gain amounting to millions of dollars annually. And most players like being in Toronto.

In addition, in recent years, Canada and Ontario have undertaken far-reaching business tax reform aimed at boosting business competitiveness. Capital taxes have been eliminated, corporate income tax rates are being reduced, and Ontario has harmonized its provincial sales tax with the federal goods and services tax. These reforms all provide positive financial benefits to Toronto-based sports franchises.

Therefore, Toronto has the right market conditions in place for the financial success of most, or all, of its pro sports franchises. The region is home to a large and growing population with high average incomes. There is a strong corporate presence. And the playing field for pro sports franchises within North America is more level than it was a decade ago.

League Competitive Conditions

The next stage is to assess the league-specific factors that affect each team. As described earlier, among the four major North American leagues, MLB makes the least effort to create a level playing field among franchises. With its soft salary-cap system and limited revenue sharing, Major League Baseball's operating rules allow a few high-revenue teams to try to buy championships year after year. Unfortunately for the Blue Jays, they play in the division with two of the biggest spenders—the New York Yankees and the Boston Red Sox—making it harder for the Jays to compete on the field while still generating positive financial results. This is one factor behind the Jays' limited competitive success since the mid-1990s.[3]

The NHL and NBA provide a more level playing field among their franchises than does MLB. The NHL and NBA have a common player entry draft, salary cap, and free agency, but only limited direct revenue sharing among franchises. Thanks to these operating rules and a strong regional market, the Maple Leafs are one of the richest franchises in the NHL. The Raptors are also profitable, and could become more so in future with improved management and team performance. In an effort to make the NBA salary cap more binding and thereby improve the financial conditions of its franchises (and, hopefully, level the competitive playing field), the NBA has demanded and obtained more contract concessions from its players. As well, the CFL, MLS, and NLL all have a salary cap or other limits on player

---

3   However, the Tampa Bay Rays face similar circumstances but have, nevertheless, succeeded in fielding highly competitive teams in recent years. So that explanation only goes so far.

salary costs. By constraining a key cost factor, leagues' competitive conditions help to support franchise financial success.

Overall, Toronto has the right market conditions in place for the financial success of its pro sports franchises—but there are major differences in how their respective leagues operate.

Franchise-Specific Factors and Toronto's Teams

In Chapter 4, we looked at three factors that can determine why some franchises succeed, while others don't. The three are:
- ownership and management;
- access to quality facilities;
- fan support.

The first franchise-specific reason why Toronto's teams succeed financially, but often come up short competitively, is related to the nature of franchise ownership. We have not done a detailed analysis of each franchise's business and competitive strategy and resulting decisions. However, it is striking that the three highest-profile Toronto franchises covered in the Forbes survey—the Leafs, Jays , and Raptors—as well as Toronto FC, are today owned by corporate entities. For these corporations, competitive results need to be good enough to maintain a minimum level of fan support, but the overall success of the franchise is measured in dollars.

Corporate-owned franchises that can generate significant revenues and profits in the large Toronto market may simply not be on the same "burning platform" as teams in other markets where financial results depend more on the team's competitive results.[4] The financial performance of most Toronto franchises is not contingent on winning.

There are, of course, differences among the franchises. Today's hard salary cap in the NHL means that a club like the Leafs can no longer try to "buy" competitive success by having payrolls that are much higher than those of other teams. A soft salary cap in MLB presents a different kind of challenge to the Blue Jays. Either they try

---

4   That said, the highly profitable Leafs franchise has been owned in past decades by private individuals—with the same mediocre results on the ice. Harold Ballard's Leafs were certainly entertaining, and they no doubt made money. But they didn't have much competitive success … and perhaps that was the plan.

to compete with the Yankees and Red Sox in terms of player payroll (a risky and possibly very costly proposition that the organization attempted to some extent in 2013, with awful results on the field), or they seek positive financial performance by fielding a less-expensive team that is still good enough to sustain interest among the fan base.

Corporate-owned franchises that can generate significant profits in the large Toronto market may simply not be the same "burning platform" as teams in other markets where financial results depend more on the team's competitive results.

As a counterpoint, the two Toronto pro sports franchises that have achieved the best competitive success in recent years—the Argos and the Rock—have been, and continue to be, owned by individuals, not corporate entities. These individuals are likely to try to balance their franchises' competitive and financial outcomes, and they make decisions on team management and player personnel accordingly. They don't want to lose money, but the results on the playing field often matter just as much as the financial performance. Of course, the balancing act can be hard to achieve. Some franchises owned by individuals experience financial losses even as the teams achieve winning records.

In all cases, franchise owners in Toronto and elsewhere cannot afford to simply ignore the feelings and commitment of their fan base—to do so would risk alienating those loyal fans. Therefore, ongoing changes in team management continue to be made in a bid to offer some hope for future competitive success. Each Toronto franchise has made changes in ownership and team management in recent years. The Maple Leafs hired a general manager in November 2008, Brian Burke, with a proven track record of success with other NHL franchises. Burke did not succeed in getting the Leafs to the playoffs, and he was fired in January 2013 and replaced by Dave Nonis. The Leafs finally did make the playoffs in the spring of 2013, and Nonis was rewarded with a five-year contract extension.

In 2009, the Blue Jays hired Alex Anthopolous as their GM, and he has been busy making significant changes aimed at turning the Jays back into legitimate contenders (albeit with very limited success so far). The Raptors sacked general manager Bryan Colangelo in the spring of 2013 and turned to Masai Ujiri, hoping that he can finally turn the team's fortunes—or misfortune—around. And Toronto FC fired its president, Kevin Payne, in September 2013 after less than a year in the job.

Perhaps the most important change in Toronto pro sports leadership was the hiring of Tim Leiweke as the president of MLSE in late April 2013. MLSE owns the Leafs, Raptors, and TFC, so hiring Leiweke away from a similar pro sports management group in Los Angeles may signal an effort by MLSE ownership to change the recent pattern of financially successful but uncompetitive teams in Toronto. Leiweke has been busy placing his stamp on the future direction of the three MLSE-owned franchises, with management changes aimed at trying to change the pattern of performance, offering Toronto's loyal sports fans some hope of competitive success … eventually.

Ultimately, a team's competitive success or failure is determined by skilful management each and every day. That means acquiring the right players through draft choices, trades, and free agent signings, with the goal of building a critical mass of talent. With or without a hard salary cap, the selection and performance of player talent is what determines a team's competitive record. Hiring the right coaches and scouts matters, too. But without the right mix of players, competitive success won't happen. Even if a corporate-owned team hires a quality general manager, the GM still has to make the right player and coaching personnel decisions. The fans have every right to question a GM's ability to lead a team to victory if that GM signs the wrong free agents or trades away fan favourites or multiple draft picks for a player that never becomes a superstar.

The lesson we draw from this is that ownership, market size, and the specific league competitive conditions are indeed factors in the business and competitive results of Toronto-based teams—but management capacity is the most significant factor in explaining why most Toronto-based franchises achieve financial success without necessarily having success on the ice or field.

The second factor for franchise success is the playing facility—and Toronto has quality pro sports facilities, all of which are attractive places to attend a game.

Lastly, all pro sports franchises need to grow and nurture a strong fan base to succeed. They need to be aware of how consumer tastes are evolving and of the changing demographics of their market. Over 40 per cent of the people living in Toronto today were not born in Canada, and its professional sports franchises must adjust to this new reality. The financial success of the Raptors and Toronto FC, despite their dismal results in the standings, may well reflect the changes in consumer tastes and Toronto's demographics.

> Toronto fans have a history of tolerating competitive mediocrity to a degree that fans in Montréal, Ottawa, and many other Canadian cities will not.

But why do fans in the Toronto region seem so willing to tolerate mediocrity? Maybe it's just a matter of simple economics. Combine strong consumer demand (a large population, with considerable individual and corporate purchasing power, fed by strong media interest) with a limited supply of available tickets for most pro sports events (especially NHL hockey), and you get sustaining fan support. Toronto is the media centre of English-speaking Canada. Sports coverage in the Toronto area is extensive, aggressive, and has fed the ongoing development of a fan base in the GTA, despite the often-mediocre athletic performance of the teams. Not all Toronto teams have the same intense fan support, of course. But Toronto fans have a history of tolerating competitive mediocrity to a degree that fans in Montréal, Ottawa, and other Canadian cities will not.

Conclusion

So why are most of Toronto's pro sports teams financial successes but competitive flops? By using the analytical structure developed in this book, we can see that the financial success of Toronto franchises is supported by local market-based factors such as population size, income levels, and head office presence. League competitive conditions are particularly important to the Blue Jays, who play in the same division as two of the biggest spenders in baseball—the Yankees and the Red Sox—and therefore do not compete on a level playing field.

However, ownership and management matter critically to franchise success, and Toronto's franchises are no exception. Four Toronto franchises that are owned by corporate entities (the Leafs, Jays, Raptors, and Toronto FC) are generally financially successful, but have produced mediocre results on the field or ice in recent years. Corporations are expected by their shareholders to achieve an adequate financial return. While competitive results need to be good enough to maintain a minimum level of fan support and profitability, corporate success is measured in dollars—not in wins.

In contrast, the Argos and the Rock have achieved competitive success in recent years and are owned by individuals. These individuals may place a different importance on their franchises' competitive and financial outcomes than would corporate owners of a team—and they would make decisions on team management and player personnel accordingly.

In short, a strong local market means there is less urgency for many Toronto teams to achieve the same success competitively as they are having financially. And unlike in smaller markets where teams may need to win in order to be financially successful, teams in Toronto can struggle on the field or ice but still be financial success stories.

Chapter 11

Fantasy Football! How Many Teams Could There Be in the Canadian Football League?

Fans of the Canadian Football League are passionate—about their teams and about their game. But could that passion be enough to support more CFL franchises?

Every November in the Canadian Football League, the Western Conference champions take on the Eastern Conference winners in the Grey Cup game, arguably Canada's most popular annual sporting event.

Amateur and professional competition for the Grey Cup dates back to 1909, but the trophy has been the sole property of the CFL since the league was officially founded in 1958. The league—which represents the highest level of football played in Canada—is also the professional sports league with the largest number of franchises in Canada at eight (soon to be nine with the entry of the Ottawa Redblacks in the 2014 season). That's more than in the National Hockey League (which has seven Canadian teams).

Still, with no teams outside Canada today, the CFL is a small league in terms of franchise numbers. That creates a problem— the teams play each other too many times, thereby diminishing the entertainment value. The CFL has two divisions—East and West—

with four teams in each in 2013. The league's regular season consists of 18 games spread over 19 weeks of play, and each team played its divisional rivals three or four times and played teams from the other division twice in 2013.

We will now use our analytical framework to evaluate whether market conditions in Canada could support an expanded CFL beyond the new Ottawa franchise. Again, going back to Chapter 2, we established that a professional sports franchise can be successful over the long run in a specific market if four market conditions are met. They are a:

- large (enough) and growing population;
- relatively wealthy market;
- sound corporate presence;
- level playing field.

Other factors—such as league operating conditions and franchise-specific factors (e.g., stable ownership)—are also important to financial success. But for the purpose of this chapter, we focus on the market conditions needed for a CFL franchise to be successful, and how many more CFL teams could the country sustain today.

CFL Market Conditions

The CFL is not one of the four major North American pro sports leagues, nor does it claim to be. The CFL is not trying to compete with the National Football League. Instead, it is a second-tier league (similar to the American Hockey League, which serves largely as a development league for the National Hockey League). Therefore, the market requirements for a successful franchise in the CFL are not the same as those of a franchise in a top-tier league. This is particularly true when it comes to two of the market pillars mentioned above—corporate presence and a level playing field. Of course, the stronger the corporate presence in a market, the better are a CFL team's chances for success. A strong corporate presence increases a team's revenues from corporate boxes and boosts sponsorship and paid advertisement.

A CFL team's revenue requirements are clearly not the same as those of an NHL franchise, principally because the player salary cap in the CFL is so much lower. The CFL salary cap was set at $4.4 million for the 2013 season. In contrast, the NHL cap for the 2013–14 season was set at $64.3 million—about 15 times more. Even if one compares the salary cap of each league per home game, the ratio would favour the CFL. At less than $500,000 per game ($4.4 million divided by nine home games), the CFL cap on a per game basis is less than a third of the NHL's, which stands at over $1.5 million per game ($64.3 million divided by 41 home games).

> The two market pillars that matter the most to the CFL are population and the relative wealth of the market.

Similarly, since the CFL has franchises only in Canada, the level playing field criterion is much less in play. With all teams located in Canada,[1] franchises in the CFL do not have to contend with issues related to the exchange rate. While many U.S.-born players (nearly 50 per cent of CFL players) were certainly unhappy when the Canadian dollar was at 62 cents U.S. in 2002 and were less likely to sign with a CFL team, the weakness or strength of the dollar does not favour any one franchise over another (unlike in the NHL, where the weak Canadian dollar made it difficult for Canadian-based teams to compete financially with U.S.-based franchises).

---

1   This wasn't always the case. In 1993, the CFL expanded into the United States. The experiment failed, and the CFL became an all-Canadian league once again in 1996. But between 1993 and 1995, seven U.S.-based franchises played at least one season in the league.

Table 9

Existing Canadian Football League Cities—Market Size and Income
(population, 000s; annual income, $)

Team	Population	Per capita disposable income
Montreal Alouettes	3,958	26,724
Toronto Argonauts	5,941	30,469
Hamilton Tiger-Cats	757	29,647
Winnipeg Blue Bombers	778	28,549
Saskatchewan Roughriders	226	36,005
Calgary Stampeders	1,309	42,870
Edmonton Eskimos	1,230	37,917
BC Lions	2,464	30,020

Note: Population and income data are for 2012. All figures are those of the census metropolitan area (CMA) where each team is located. The figures used for the Saskatchewan Roughriders are those for the Regina CMA, while those used for the BC Lions are the Vancouver CMA numbers. Sources: The Conference Board of Canada; Statistics Canada.

The two market pillars that matter the most to the CFL are population and the relative wealth of the market. Table 9 shows how the eight current CFL franchises stacked up with respect to these two criteria in 2012.

The smallest market is that of the Saskatchewan Roughriders, with Regina at 226,000 people. The Roughriders are a highly successful franchise, so it could be argued that the minimum market size required to support a CFL team is as low as 226,000.

But we don't believe that a market of 226,000 is itself sufficient to support a CFL franchise. The Saskatchewan Roughriders, while located in Regina, are properly named—the team benefits from the support of the entire province, and even that of Saskatchewan natives living outside the province. (As a measure of Saskatchewan natives' loyalty to the Roughriders, simply count the number of green Rider jerseys in the stands at away games, particularly in Calgary and Edmonton!) So we don't think that there could soon be a game between, for example, Regina and Saskatoon—adding a second franchise in Saskatchewan would divide a unique market and place one or both franchises at risk.

This prompts the question: If 226,000 is too low, what is the minimum population required to sustain a CFL franchise? The second-smallest CFL market is Hamilton, with a population of 757,000. If this is the minimum population required, only Ottawa–Gatineau and Québec City can be viewed as potential expansion markets. However, we think that at least four other markets—Kitchener, London, Halifax, and Moncton—should be considered. That means six markets (including Ottawa, which is getting a CFL team in 2014) are potential candidates for expansion in the near term.

Ottawa–Gatineau

At almost 1.3 million people, the Ottawa–Gatineau CMA should never have lost its CFL franchise. The national capital is slated to get a team again. After repeated delays and setbacks in the franchise- and stadium-approval processes, the return of the CFL to Ottawa is now set for the 2014 season, once Lansdowne Park has been renovated. Once the Redblacks take the field, the CFL will again be a nine-team league.

Québec City

With a population of 770,000, Québec City would appear to be next in line for a CFL franchise. It is already home to one of the most successful teams in Canadian Interuniversity Sport (CIS) football, the Laval University Rouge et Or. The Québec City economy has been one of the best-performing municipal economies east of Saskatchewan over the past decade, pushing per capita disposable income of the CMA past that of Montréal and Winnipeg. Moreover, Québec City already has a football stadium. PEPS (Pavillon de l'éducation physique et des sports) stadium officially seats a little over 12,500. But on many occasions, nearly 20,000 fans have packed themselves in for an important Rouge et Or match. While the stadium would require a bit of work to meet the needs of a CFL team on a permanent basis, it provides a sound starting point.

However, all of the CMA's current efforts to attract a professional sports franchise are being concentrated on bringing the NHL back to the city. For now, Québec City should not be viewed as a priority CFL market. But if the city is successful in its bid to bring NHL hockey back to Québec City, and if it shows that it can support that team, that could put a different perspective on whether a CFL team could flourish there as well. One key issue is whether the Québec City market would be overstretched with both an NHL and a CFL team. But there is only a partial overlap in the CFL and NHL seasons; and given the incredible success of the Rouge et Or, Québec City must be considered as a potential CFL market over the long term.

Although Québec City would appear to be second in line for a franchise, it should not be viewed as a priority market for now.

Kitchener–Cambridge–Waterloo and London

These two Ontario markets are grouped together as they are similar in size, with the population in each CMA now surpassing the 500,000 mark. Both are home to CIS football teams, and both have long and successful football traditions. With respect to per capita disposable income, Kitchener–Cambridge–Waterloo (KCW) ranks well, with a level of $29,082 in 2012. That is higher than Winnipeg or Montréal. Per capita disposable income in London stood at $27,405 in 2012, lower than that of any of the markets currently in the CFL and 22nd among Canada's 28 largest CMAs.

In terms of possible playing facilities, however, London possesses an advantage. TD Waterhouse Stadium, home of the Western Ontario Mustangs, can seat 8,000 people. While this capacity is clearly not sufficient for a CFL franchise, the Montreal Alouettes took about 10 years to renovate and reshape the aging but revered Percival

Molson Stadium into a CFL-worthy facility with seating capacity of 25,000. A major investment would be required to expand London's facilities, but TD Waterhouse Stadium provides a foundation to build upon.

The same does not hold true for KCW. While there are three football stadiums in the CMA (two of which are used by CIS football teams), all three are small and would require a large investment to expand or rebuild to reach the 25,000 or more in seating capacity required for a CFL franchise. Kitchener's Centennial Stadium seats just 3,200 spectators (but, on the plus side, does have easy highway access from Waterloo, Guelph, and Cambridge). University Stadium in Waterloo seats 6,000 and is home to the Wilfred Laurier Golden Hawks. Warrior Field—home of the University of Waterloo Warriors—is new but has a capacity of just 5,400, including seating for 1,400 in the grandstand.

Given the much larger investment that would be required to build a CFL-suitable stadium in the KCW area, and given the relatively close distance to Hamilton and Toronto with their CFL teams, the London CMA has the edge when it comes to its potential as a new market for the CFL. But both London and KCW have their limitations and would be long shots to win or maintain franchises.

One other factor regarding the establishment of an additional CFL franchise in Southern Ontario is potential market saturation. There are already two CFL teams in Southern Ontario (Hamilton and Toronto), and residents of the region can also drive to Buffalo to watch the Bills of the National Football League (or they can catch the Bills in Toronto, where the team plays one regular-season game each year). And based on the uneven support for the two existing franchises, it is not certain that the Southern Ontario market could support any more CFL teams.

Halifax and Moncton

Two other potential CFL markets are located in Canada's Atlantic provinces. Atlantic Canada does not currently have a top-tier professional sports franchise, despite the obvious appetite for sports in the area. But to support a franchise, a region needs more than just an appetite for pro sports. With a population of slightly more than 410,000 people, Halifax would be a relatively small urban market for the CFL. Still, the Saskatchewan Roughriders have shown that a team with provincial and regional reach can be successful, and a Halifax-based franchise could become a team for the entire Maritimes. The biggest challenge for Halifax is the lack of a CFL-quality facility. Huskies Stadium at St. Mary's University can seat up to 11,000 fans, as it did in 2005 when the stadium hosted an exhibition game between the Hamilton Tiger-Cats and the Toronto Argonauts and temporary stands were constructed for the event. (The "Touchdown Atlantic" game was aimed at gauging the region's public support for a CFL franchise.) However, on a permanent basis, the stadium seats only 4,000 people. Given the physical space constraints, a major expansion of Huskies Stadium would be very difficult. Therefore, a significant investment would be required to create a CFL-ready stadium in the Halifax area.

Moncton must also be considered as a potential new CFL market in Atlantic Canada. This New Brunswick CMA is home to 143,000 residents, making it even smaller than Regina (though Moncton's population is growing rapidly). However, the city has gained the nickname of "Hub City" because of its central location in the region and because Moncton has historically been the railway and land transportation hub for the Atlantic provinces. With its central location, a team based in Moncton could benefit from the support of the entire province of New Brunswick (with a population of more than 750,000) and much of the rest of Atlantic Canada.

The city has a playing facility that is almost CFL-ready—Moncton Stadium, located on the campus of l'Université de Moncton. Originally built to host the 2010 world junior track and field championships, the stadium has 10,000 permanent seats, and is expandable to a 20,725 capacity via temporary seating. The stadium hosted the first CFL regular season game in the Maritimes (again called "Touchdown Atlantic") in September 2010. Regular season CFL games were played there in 2011 and 2013.

While Moncton Stadium would require some work to bring it permanently up to CFL standards, it gives Moncton an edge over Halifax in being the location for a CFL franchise for Atlantic Canada. Still, neither the Moncton nor the Halifax market alone is large enough to ensure long-term viability of a CFL team. If a franchise does come to the Maritimes, its owners will have to work hard to market the team as a regional franchise—one that can attract fans from the neighbouring provinces as well, and do so on an ongoing basis.

Conclusion

Our market analysis indicates that there is room for more than eight teams in the Canadian Football League. Ottawa will join in 2014, and cities such as London and Moncton could be contenders. If positioned and marketed as regional teams, both London and Moncton have the required market size, as well as stadiums that could be expanded to become permanent CFL facilities.

Adding Ottawa, London, and Moncton would lift the number of teams in the CFL from eight to eleven. As for Québec City, the focus for now is solely on bringing the NHL's Nordiques back. But the CFL could be the next step for this community over the longer term. That would increase the total number of teams to twelve.

While we believe the CFL could have as many as twelve teams in the near term, the expansion will not happen overnight. And the issue of ownership is critical. Even in a good market, strong ownership is key to a franchise. Finding dedicated owners for each additional CFL franchise will be key to the long-term success of any new franchise.

Still, there is considerable room for growth in the CFL. A CFL of ten or twelve teams would be much more entertaining for fans, and would create new regional rivalries that don't exist today.

An expanded CFL—one that grew step by step—could have a bright future.

Chapter 12
How Many NHL Franchises Could Canada Sustain?

Canadians have a seemingly insatiable appetite for hockey. But is that appetite enough to support more NHL teams in this country? And if so, where would the new franchises be most likely to succeed?

Canadians are passionate about their sports. And one sport in particular is at the top of that list—hockey! In this chapter, we look at the question of how many more National Hockey League teams Canada could support.

Today, Winnipeg is once again home to an NHL franchise. And Québec City has a serious business plan in place (including the construction of a new arena at a current estimated cost of $400 million) to bring the NHL back to that city. But if Québec City does succeed in getting a team, is that where Canadian expansion ends? Or could the country support even more NHL franchises?

Using our analytical toolkit, we answer this question.

The Four Market Pillars

In Chapter 2, we listed the four pillars of success for a professional sport franchise, which we have used throughout this book. We turn to these pillars once again to identify potential new NHL markets in Canada.

Pillar 1: Population Size

For a community to support a professional sport franchise over the long term, there must be a sufficient and growing population base. A community that is home to 50,000 diehard hockey fans would not be big enough to sustain an NHL franchise. (Conversely, even in a local market with a population of 10 million or more, if that market has little passion for hockey, a franchise will not be successful.)

Prior to the 2011–12 season, all NHL franchises in Canada were located in markets with a population base of over 1 million. The return of the Jets to Winnipeg has changed that benchmark, since the population of the Winnipeg census metropolitan area (CMA) stood at 778,000 in 2012.

> For NHL hockey, with 41 regular-season home games—many of them played on cold, snowy winter nights during the week—it is not realistic to think that fans would drive from all over the province on a regular basis to cheer on their team.

The team has made a great start financially, selling out its available season tickets for years to come, thanks to massive pent-up demand. Still, the basic economics of pro sports apply. Winnipeg is at the lower threshold of population size when it comes to supporting an NHL franchise. Any Canadian market with a population under 750,000 would find it very difficult to sustain an NHL franchise over the longer term and thus should be excluded from the list of potential NHL markets. Given this threshold, there are only two potential new NHL markets in Canada: Québec City and Hamilton. These two CMAs posted head counts of 770,000 and 757,000 in 2012, respectively. More importantly, the population levels in both of these markets have been rising steadily for years and are expected to continue to do so.

In the previous chapter, we discussed whether a smaller city could get by in the CFL by representing and drawing upon fans from across a province or region, rather than a city. That arrangement already works for Regina and the Saskatchewan Roughriders, and it could work for Moncton or Halifax in Atlantic Canada. However, in our view it wouldn't work for an NHL franchise. For the CFL, people might reasonably drive up to 300 kilometres (or three hours) to attend nine home games of the provincial or regional pro football team, with most of the games played on summer and fall weekends. But for NHL hockey, with 41 regular-season home games—many of them played on cold, snowy winter nights during the week—it is not realistic to think that fans would drive from all over the province or region on a regular basis to cheer on their team.

Pillar 2: Market Wealth

Our second pillar is the wealth of the market. This pillar has grown in importance, given the rapid rise in ticket prices for professional sport events over the past 20 years. Personal disposable income per capita in Winnipeg in 2012 was $29,549. This put Winnipeg in 17th place among Canada's 28 largest census metropolitan areas—but still ahead of Montréal among Canadian census metropolitan areas that are home to NHL franchises. What about Québec City and Hamilton? Québec City was ranked 15th in 2012 and Hamilton was ranked 13th—both above Winnipeg and Montréal. Therefore, based on market wealth, Québec City and Hamilton are two potential sites for NHL franchises.

Pillar 3: Corporate Presence

In Chapter 7, a relatively small corporate presence was highlighted as an issue for Winnipeg and, particularly, for Québec City when these teams moved away in the mid-1990s. By 2012, the situation had not changed much—of Canada's 800 largest corporations, only 26 had head offices located in Winnipeg. Even fewer—14—were located in Québec City. That is a far cry from the levels in Toronto (253),

Calgary (135), Montréal (97), or Vancouver (94). However, Edmonton and Ottawa are home to NHL franchises, and Edmonton had just 22 corporate head offices in 2012, while Ottawa had 18. This suggests that while a strong corporate presence is desirable, it is hard to dismiss Québec City as a potential NHL market simply because of a low corporate presence. Moreover, corporations located across the province of Québec would likely show interest in supporting an NHL franchise in the city. Also, keep in mind that Montréal, with 97 head offices, is just 200 kilometres away from Québec City.

Where does Hamilton stand when it comes to corporate presence? Hamilton was home to the head office of only eight of Canada's 800 largest corporations in 2009. While this is a strike against it, Hamilton has the huge benefit of being located near Toronto, where 253 large corporations have their head offices. A new NHL franchise in Hamilton could likely count on the support of at least some of the large corporations based in the Greater Toronto Area. Therefore, Hamilton qualifies as a potential NHL market in terms of corporate presence.

Pillar 4: A Level Playing Field

The playing field has rarely been more level for Canadian franchises playing in North American professional sport leagues. The Canadian dollar has been within 10 cents of parity with the U.S. greenback since 2007, and The Conference Board of Canada expects that it will remain there for the foreseeable future. This is in sharp contrast to 2002, when the Canadian dollar bottomed out at just under US$0.62. A chronically strong loonie is a tremendous help for Canadian franchises that play in the major North American leagues, where teams' largest expense—players' salaries—are denominated in U.S. dollars. Also, taxes on individuals and corporations have been reduced by the federal government and several provincial governments over the past decade, reducing or eliminating the tax spread with U.S. jurisdictions—welcome news for Canadian franchises.

Overall

Based on a review of our four market pillars, Québec City and Hamilton are the only two potential new Canadian markets for the NHL.

Competitive Conditions of the NHL

In Chapter 3, we introduced the fundamental issue of whether pro sports leagues make an adequate effort to level the playing field among their teams. On this issue, the National Football League is in a league of its own, sharing up to 80 per cent of overall revenues. At the other end of the spectrum lies Major League Baseball, with a soft salary cap system under which a team with a $45-million payroll must try to compete against teams with $220-million payrolls— a very unlevel playing field. The NHL lies somewhere between these two extremes. It has a player entry draft, a hard salary cap, and free agency. And it also introduced more revenue sharing among franchises as part of its 2013 collective agreement with its players. But even with enhanced revenue sharing, the NHL faces a chronic challenge in terms of keeping its weaker franchises afloat, competitively as well as economically.

> Owning a successful sport franchise is all about long-term commitment. Obtaining a franchise in order to do a quick asset flip is a recipe for disaster.

Overall, the NHL has become a much more welcoming circuit for smaller markets since the 2005 collective bargaining agreement with the players came into effect. Even more progress on that front has been made with the 2013 agreement. The key measure in the 2005 agreement—the salary cap—ensures that teams in smaller markets (such as Winnipeg) won't be grossly outspent by those in larger markets (such as Toronto). The 2013 collective agreement added more sharing of revenues among the franchises. These two factors make Québec City and Hamilton legitimate contenders for new NHL franchises.

Ownership, Facility, and Fan Support

Even under the best local market and league conditions, professional sport franchises can still fail if:

- ownership makes bad decisions and does not provide its fan base with the best possible product;
- the playing facility is not adequate;
- the franchise does not understand the demographic evolution of its market.

Owning a successful sport franchise is all about long-term commitment. Obtaining a franchise in order to do a quick asset flip is a recipe for disaster. Responsible ownership would be key to the success of NHL franchises in Hamilton or Québec City.

An adequate playing facility is a must for success. Originally, Copps Coliseum, which is owned by the City of Hamilton, was built in the hope that Hamilton could draw an NHL franchise. Construction started in 1983, and the arena was completed in 1985 at a cost of $33.5 million. The facility has a seating capacity of a little over 17,000. Is the arena still NHL-adequate? The NHL business model has evolved greatly since 1985. Arenas have grown in size, and corporate boxes have become increasingly important. Copps Coliseum would likely need considerable renovating and upgrading before the NHL would agree to place a franchise in Hamilton. Still, the facility provides a good starting point.

When Jim Balsillie, the former co-CEO of Research In Motion (RIM, now called BlackBerry), tried to bring an NHL team to Canada, he considered putting it in the Kitchener–Cambridge–Waterloo (KCW) area. That's where RIM's headquarters were located. But more importantly, KCW is outside the territories that belong, under NHL franchise rules, to the Toronto Maple Leafs and Buffalo Sabres. Establishing a team in KCW would therefore avoid the fuss of a territorial battle. The question then becomes, which business proposition is the less costly? On the one hand, by establishing the team in Hamilton, the owner would have to buy out the territorial rights but would not have the cost of building an arena from the ground up. On the other hand, by establishing a team in KCW, the owner would avoid the territorial battle but would have to build a new arena from scratch. Overall, the Hamilton option remains the best one, based on costs and also because of Hamilton's closer proximity to Toronto's large market and corporations.

The situation is different in Québec City, where the state of Le Colisée was one of the reasons why the Nordiques moved to Denver in 1995. Therefore, to bring the Nordiques back, the construction of a new building was required. Toward that goal, the City of Québec grabbed the bull by the horns and got the project under way. The construction of a new NHL-quality building should be completed in 2015, even though the NHL has made no commitment to bring a team back to Québec City.

In both Hamilton and Québec City, NHL-worthy facilities are either just a renovation project away or are on the way—strengthening these two cities' position as the only two potential new NHL markets.

Two Teams in One Market?

Could any single market in Canada support two NHL franchises? When this question arises, three markets—Montréal, Toronto, and Vancouver—come to mind.

At almost 2.5 million people, Vancouver is triple the minimum size required to support an NHL franchise. So, could it support two? Probably not. The Vancouver market is still too small to be home to a second NHL franchise, since the risk of market saturation would be too high.

Montréal once had two NHL franchises (the other was called the Maroons), but that was over half a century ago. Today, Montréal is home to almost 4 million people, but the Montréal region has been grappling with a relatively underperforming economy for decades. Indeed, average annual real economic growth in Montréal has been below 2 per cent over the past 25 years. As a result, Montréal's per capita disposable income has slid steadily in the rankings and stood 24th among Canada's 28 largest urban centres in 2012. Moreover, we are talking about Montréal—home of the storied Canadiens with their

24 Stanley Cup championships and long history. It is hard to imagine any individual or corporation investing millions of dollars to try to compete with the Canadiens on their own turf.

Table 10
Total Fan Requirement in Toronto

Team	Number of home games (including pre-season)	Fans per game	Total population requirement
Toronto Blue Jays	81	30,334	2,457,054
Toronto Raptors	45	17,319	779,355
Toronto Maple Leafs	45	17,122	770,490
Toronto Argonauts	10	23,441	234,410
Toronto FC	19	17,870	339,530
Toronto Rock	9	9,723	87,507
Total			**4,668,346**

Sources: ESPN; Canadian Football League; Major League Soccer; National Lacrosse League; Statistics Canada; The Conference Board of Canada.

That leaves the census metropolitan area of Toronto. Based on the first of our four pillars, population size, the city would have a tough time supporting two NHL teams due to market saturation.

How do we reach that conclusion? In 2012, the population of the Toronto census metropolitan area stood at 5.9 million people. Toronto is already home to a Major League Baseball team, a National Basketball Association team, a National Hockey League team, a Canadian Football League team, a Major League Soccer team, and a National Lacrosse League team. When we add up the fan requirements for each of these teams (see Table 10), there does seem to be room at first glance for one more NHL franchise in the Toronto CMA. However, Toronto is also home to many other regular sporting events, including Ultimate Fighting Championship (UFC) events, the Honda Indy Toronto car race, the Rogers Cup tennis tournament,

Buffalo Bills games, occasional professional golf tournaments, and other special events. Adding all these pro sports events to the total changes the picture substantially.

Getting and keeping a second NHL team in Toronto would be difficult.

One of the obstacles standing in the way of a second NHL team in Toronto is a new arena. Overcoming that obstacle could be difficult, as evidenced by the debate that raged over the funding of a new Markham facility. But there are two other factors to consider; the acquisition cost or expansion fee, and the paying of a territorial fee to the Toronto Maple Leafs (and perhaps the Buffalo Sabres). These factors remain huge obstacles. Moreover, the prospective owner of a second Toronto NHL team would have to negotiate market entry with the combined new Maple Leaf Sports and Entertainment (MLSE) ownership group that now includes both Bell and Rogers. These large communications and media organizations acquired the Leafs' corporate owner, MLSE, in order to maximize Toronto sports content for their various media platforms. A second NHL team in Toronto would represent even more media content and would further complicate the already complex negotiations on who gets to broadcast what.

Given all these factors, getting and keeping a second NHL team in Toronto, at this point in time, would be difficult.

Conclusion

The Canada of today could sustain a maximum of nine NHL franchises—a conclusion based on our analysis of the market conditions required to support an NHL-level professional hockey team today. And while Hamilton and Québec City do appear to be viable locations for future NHL franchises, they are all at the lower limit. (In fact, we believe that Winnipeg is at the lower limit as well.) These markets have only the minimum market size and income, and a relatively small number of corporate head offices. They would need the

Canadian dollar to at least remain relatively healthy. As well, these smaller markets will always be more exposed than their larger competitors to any negative shocks to the national economy or to their community.

Yes, they could be successful in the NHL—but only if they have dedicated owners who are in it for the long run and who manage their business operations carefully.

Chapter 13

In Team Pro Sports, NFL "Socialism" Is the Big Winner for Owners and Fans

If pro sports leagues are evaluated as economic systems, which ones are the most "capitalist"? That is, which are the ones where individual interests are paramount? On the other side of the coin, which leagues are the most "socialist" ones, where the emphasis is on shared economic interests? And which produce the strongest performances? The results may surprise you.

In this chapter, we take a system-wide look at pro sports leagues and teams, using a comparative economic systems approach. We consider which economic system—from highly socialist to purely capitalist— best describes their operations, and we identify the top performers.

The "Socialist" NFL

Capitalist America's most popular pro sports league—The National Football League—is also by far the most "socialist" of the major pro sports leagues in North America today. More than 80 per cent of league and club revenues are shared among the franchises. TV broadcast revenues, currently about $5 billion annually, are shared equally among the franchises, as are merchandising revenues. Even gate revenues are shared between the home and visiting teams, with 40 per cent of the ticket revenues for each game going to the visiting team. The NFL also has a "hard" salary cap. A firm upper limit on annual player salaries is set at between 47 and 48 per cent of league revenues, using a complex formula that takes into account all revenue sources. For 2013, the salary cap was $123 million, up from $120 in 2012.

NFL owners understand that they have a common interest in maximizing total revenue, sharing it widely, and controlling costs. Franchise values have risen significantly over the decades. Most franchises now exceed $1 billion in value, with a few (such as the Dallas Cowboys) approaching $2 billion. And they all make lots of money.

> The NFL's operating rules achieve both financial success for its franchises and balanced competitive conditions for its fans.

Overall, the resulting on-field competitive conditions in the NFL are exceptionally balanced. The combination of a hard salary cap and significant revenue sharing means that almost every NFL team has a reasonable expectation of making the playoffs each year. Teams' qualification and positioning for the playoffs are often determined on the final weekend(s) of the season, keeping fan interest high. As a result, management quality and player performance have become the dominant factors that determine team performance.

In short, the NFL's operating rules achieve both financial success for its franchises and balanced competitive conditions for its fans. The Super Bowl provides an annual marquee event to showcase the game, but the underlying business model determines the league's ongoing success.

There is one obvious major exception to all this socialism in the NFL—the treatment of individual players, which is distinctly market-driven. Under the defined salary cap, teams are ready to pay massive salaries to attract stars, and few superstars ever actually hit the open market. But teams are equally ready to discard players when they are no longer useful or are deemed too expensive for their current level of play. Thus, the NFL has a very capitalist attitude toward its players.

Having said that, the NFL responded to the recent threat of a lawsuit by current and former NFL players over head trauma with a proposed out-of-court settlement worth $765 million—an important concession from the owners toward the players. A U.S. federal judge deemed this amount to be potentially too low, and has asked for more financial information before finalizing. While this proposed settlement was hardly an act of socialism, it is more than the National Hockey League has done for its players.

Major League Soccer: In Transition

A rising star among North America's pro sports leagues is Major League Soccer, or MLS. The original business model was decidedly collectivist, based on cost control and steady growth. Rather than a league based on individual franchises, MLS was founded in 1993 as a single entity that controlled all player contracts and costs under a tight salary cap and shared the profits or, until recently, the losses. Three entrepreneurial sports businessmen—Lamar Hunt, Phil Anschutz, and Robert Craft—kept the league afloat through its early days and de facto controlled many of the early franchises.

After some growing pains, MLS is catching on with sports fans across North America. The MLS model, which has taken a great leap forward in recent years, is based on attracting new owners with significant financial capacity, adding franchises in soccer-friendly markets, creating soccer-specific stadiums, and attracting some high-profile European stars, including David Beckham and Thierry Henry. A salary cap of approximately $2.95 million in aggregate and about $350,000 per player (and lower for players early in their careers) was in place for 2013, but teams are able to sign and compensate designated star players at a market-determined rate, with a hit to the salary cap that is limited to the defined per player maximum. The step-by-step addition of three strong Canadian franchises (Toronto FC, Vancouver Whitecaps, and Montréal Impact) with already-developed fan support has been a significant boost to the league, as has adding teams in the soccer-friendly markets of Seattle, Portland, and Philadelphia.

Where the MLS goes next is open to debate, but the league is clearly in transition—from a cost-controlling single entity that shared the start-up losses to a league driven by star players, strong owners, and the maximizing of revenues from growing media exposure and ticket sales.

The NHL: A Mixed Economy

Moving from left to right along the economic spectrum, the National Hockey League is next. Like the NFL, the NHL has a hard salary cap to control overall player salary costs, set at $64.3 million for the 2013–14 season. The salary cap will be set at 50 per cent of league revenues, as based on the previous season, starting from the 2014–15 season onwards. (There is also a player salary floor, which obliges all teams to spend enough to ensure they are able to put a competitive team on the ice. The floor is $44 million for 2013–14.) It took a labour dispute that washed out the first half of the 2012–13 NHL season to reduce the players' share of revenues from 57 per cent in the 2005 bargaining agreement, to 50 per cent in the 2013 agreement. The good news for fans is that this latest collective bargaining agreement doesn't expire until 2022, which means they can breathe more easily for a while to come.

The 2103 collective bargaining agreement also revised the NHL's revenue-sharing arrangements. In a nutshell, the new revenue-sharing system takes a designated amount of revenue from the strongest revenue-generating teams and shares it among the weakest ones, with the percentages based on the overall revenues of the NHL. Using the 2011–12 hockey-related revenue figure of $3.3 billion, the league multiplies this amount by 0.06055 to determine the amount of revenues to be shared among teams. Using that formula, the revenues to be shared would be $200 million.

Under the new system, the top 10 revenue-generating teams can pay no more than 50 per cent of the revenues to be shared. Again, using the 2011–12 numbers, the top 10 teams would contribute no more than $100 million combined to the pot. Moreover, the contribution of each of the top 10 teams is based on how much they earn over and above the 11th-ranked team, so the teams in the eighth to tenth spots in terms of revenue would pay a much smaller amount than the top three revenue-generating teams.

In addition, teams taking part in the Stanley Cup playoffs will now share 35 per cent of their ticket revenues for each home playoff game, regardless of their revenue-generating capacity during the regular season.

If the total target amount has not been raised after these two phases of revenue sharing ($200 million from our numerical example above), the NHL will contribute the balance using the league's centrally generated revenues.

The intent of the revenue-sharing system is to allow the weakest revenue-generating teams to afford a player payroll that is somewhere between the salary floor and salary cap. The revision of the NHL revenue-sharing system eliminated some of the barriers that had prevented teams from receiving funds in the past. For example, under the old model, teams in large media markets (such as the New York Islanders and Anaheim Ducks) were prevented outright from receiving funds. Now, teams in media markets of more than 3 million households can still receive half of what the calculations would otherwise dictate. In addition, various performance parameters (including average paid attendance of at least 14,000) have been removed. In the past, failing to meet those criteria could cause a team to lose up to half of its possible revenues. Although it removes these barriers, the 2013 collective bargaining agreement now requires weaker revenue-generating teams to submit business plans on how they will improve their financial performance and thereby reduce their need for future revenue transfers.

The NHL is willing to provide subsidies to its weaker franchises in order to protect the current and future value of the stronger franchises, since the bankruptcy of any franchise is not a good signal to prospective investors. As history has shown, the NHL will also move to recover its paid-out subsidies if a subsidized franchise changes ownership. When the NHL franchise in Atlanta moved to Winnipeg in May 2011, for example, around $60 million of the $170 million purchase price reportedly went back to the NHL.

> In the NHL, management quality and player performance play a central role in deciding who succeeds and who fails.

Overall, the on-ice competitive conditions in the NHL are good, as can be seen in the fact that a financially weak franchise, the New York Islanders, made the playoffs in 2012–13, while a financially strong franchise, the Philadelphia Flyers, did not. Hockey is a game that requires a full team effort to achieve success. Having and making money is no guarantee of victory, and the salary cap and salary floor create a similar operating space for each team. Management quality and player performance play a central role in deciding who succeeds and who fails.

The Modern Capitalism of the NBA and Major League Baseball

The NBA

So far, the National Basketball Association (NBA) has been less market-interventionist than the NHL. It has a "soft" salary cap that sets a limit on a team's player compensation, but the NBA salary cap system also includes an array of significant and arcane exemptions that allow teams to exceed the defined salary cap. Until recently the

NBA did not share locally generated revenue among teams, but it did share the proceeds of a luxury tax on teams that exceeded the salary cap, and it shared the revenues from national TV broadcasting rights.

According to Forbes 2013 team valuations, 22 of the 30 NBA teams made money in 2011–12. Teams in major markets, such as Los Angeles, Chicago, and New York, can sustain high ticket prices and pull in significant regional TV earnings, so they are profitable. Some teams, however, are facing ongoing challenges, with Memphis, Portland, Charlotte, and Atlanta all reported to have lost more than $10 million each in 2011–12.

To begin addressing this financial imbalance among franchises, the NBA decided in 2011 to take on its players and cut operating costs. The result was a lockout that saw the first 16 games of the 82-game regular season schedule wiped out in 2011–12. An agreement on a new salary cap level was eventually reached with the players' association in late November and ratified in early December, reducing the players' share of league revenues from 57 to 51 per cent. As a transition measure, the dollar amount of the salary cap was kept at $58 million for 2012–13 and increased slightly to $58.7 for the 2013–14 season. A higher luxury tax is also being levied on teams that exceed the salary cap.

On-floor competitive conditions in the NBA today are not as strong as those in the NFL or NHL, due to league operating rules and to the nature of the game, where a few stars can dominate.

The NBA has also entered the world of more revenue sharing. The 2013–2014 season saw the creation of a revenue-sharing pool of roughly $140 million. This pool will be allocated using a complex formula that shifts some of the financial wealth of the big-market NBA teams to the league's neediest ones. Each recipient could receive up to $16 million a year as part of the plan. This system is an important step toward improving the competitive balance within the league.

Overall, the on-floor competitive conditions in the NBA today are not as strong as those in the NFL or NHL, but the league seems to be working on the issue. In the NBA, due to the nature of the game, just a few stars working together can dominate. The championship series invariably includes a team from one of the traditionally strong markets. While the Lakers, Celtics, and Bulls have been in the final many times, the competitive success of the small-market San Antonio Spurs over the past decade is the exception that proves the rule. The Miami Heat are the latest NBA team to make use of a soft salary cap system to stack a team with superstars, including LeBron James (widely acknowledged as the best player today) who led the Heat to championships in 2012 and again in 2013.

Major League Baseball

Arguably the most "capitalist" pro sports league in North America is Major League Baseball. MLB has a much freer market for player talent than the other leagues, which drives up player costs and makes the smaller market teams largely uncompetitive on the field. Rising TV revenues for the large markets is the key source of revenue, and MLB shares enough of these revenues among its teams to ensure that it has adequate competition on the field to maintain fan interest in the game—but not enough to create the kind of level playing field we see in the NFL.

Under MLB's "soft" salary cap system, a progressive "luxury tax" is paid by a team when its player payroll exceeds the league's annual defined maximum. In 2013, the cap was set at $178 million— far beyond the revenue-generating capacity and the total player compensation of nearly every team in MLB. The New York Yankees have paid 95 per cent of the luxury tax collected to date, but the actual amount paid by the club is small relative to the massive annual revenues the Yankees are able to generate. In 2013, the Yankees reportedly paid over $29 million in luxury tax while pulling in revenues approaching $500 million.

As highlighted in Chapter 6, however, the Yankees are about to change their strategy. Since the Yankees are repeat offenders, they pay the maximum tax rate—50 per cent. But if the Yankees can bring their payroll down below the luxury tax limit for one year, they get to start all over again with a clean slate. With the luxury tax limit increasing to $189 million in 2014, rumour has it that the Yankees plan to bring their payroll below this amount, allowing them to pay the tax rate paid by first-time offenders—17 per cent—the next time they bring their payroll over the limit. Such a reduction in the tax rate means $10 million or more in savings. Had they paid a 17 per cent tax rate in 2013, the Yankees' luxury tax bill would have been a little below $10 million rather than $29 million.

Given all this free spending, it is no wonder that in November 2011, the MLB Players Association quietly signed an agreement with the owners extending their collective bargaining agreement to 2016!

In MLB, the playing field is not level, but modest revenue sharing allows smaller market teams to make money if they keep their player costs under control.

The absence of a hard salary cap as a share of expected revenues has led to enormous differences in MLB's team payrolls, severely limiting the ability of the low-payroll teams to compete on the field on a regular basis with the league's big spenders. In 2013, 14 of the 30 teams had payrolls that exceeded $100 million. (See Table 11.) The Yankees' exceptional revenue-generating capacity (over $470 million a year and growing) allows them to compete aggressively in the free-agent market each off-season, but other teams are also in the race for talent.

At the opposite end of the scale, the Houston Astros spent $24.3 million on player compensation in 2013 (meaning the Yankees paid more luxury tax than the entire Houston payroll). The Toronto Blue Jays spent $118.2 million on players, ranking the team tenth in MLB. This was a change for the Blue Jays, which used to be a "middle of the pack" spender. Unfortunately for the Jays and their fans, the gamble of increasing the payroll did not pay off in 2013.

Table 11
2013 MLB Team Payrolls Exceeding $100 Million
($ millions)

1	New York Yankees	$228,995,945
2	Los Angeles Dodgers	$216,302,909
3	Philadelphia Phillies	$159,578,214
4	Boston Red Sox	$158,967,286
5	Detroit Tigers	$149,046,84
6	San Francisco Giants	$142,180,333
7	Los Angeles Angels	$142,165,250
8	Texas Rangers	$127,197,575
9	Chicago White Sox	$124,065,277
10	Toronto Blue Jays	$118,244,039
11	St. Louis Cardinals	$116,702,085
12	Washington Nationals	$112,431,770
13	Cincinnati Reds	$110,565,728
14	Chicago Cubs	$104,150,726

Source: ESPN.

On the other side of the ledger, there are huge differences among teams in terms of their capacity to generate revenue. According to Forbes, the Yankees pulled in $471 million in revenues in 2012, while the Tampa Bay Rays managed to generate $167 million. Still, looking at the bottom line, most MLB teams regularly show profits year after year. So it is fair to surmise that even the poorest MLB teams can make money most seasons. And if local authorities can be convinced to build a new baseball-only stadium to keep a team in their city, that usually leads to an increase in the number of paying fans at games, at least until the novelty of the new stadium wears off.

How is it possible for the weaker-market teams to succeed? It's because MLB has a revenue-sharing agreement in place (albeit a modest one), under which teams share 34 per cent of their local revenues. The plan will never turn lower-revenue-generating teams into high-revenue-generating ones, but it does allow teams to become competitive if they are well-managed. A great example of that is the 2013 Pittsburgh Pirates. Almost a decade ago, the Pirates' new management team put a plan in place, beginning with the reconstruction of a farm system. All-star Andrew McCutchen was their first-round pick in 2005 and the Pirates chose to keep him within their system, giving him a six-year, $51.5 million extension in March 2012. (True, there were some busts along the way. But that happens to all teams as they try to make educated guesses on which players coming out of high school and college will be stars or, at least, regulars in "the show" and which will not.)

More recently, the Pirates began to spend during free-agency periods and to use the trade market to acquire talent. For the first time in a long while, the Pirates were buyers—not sellers—at the trade deadline in both 2012 and 2013. The revenue-sharing system, combined with effective management, helped the Pirates make the post-season in 2013 after a 20-year drought.

The key revenue differentiator among MLB teams is the richness of their local TV contracts. We have already noted the significant and growing revenues generated by the Yankees. But a number of other MLB teams are also signing very lucrative long-term TV deals, which in turn are driving up franchise values in those top-tier TV markets. For example, the Los Angeles Angels signed a $3-billion, 20-year TV contract in 2012 (or $150 million in revenue annually), and used some of the money to sign free agent Albert Pujols at $25 million per year. Teams like the Texas Rangers and San Diego Padres have signed TV deals exceeding $1 billion, which allow them to become bigger players in the free-agent market. And in March 2012, the Los Angeles Dodgers were sold to an ownership group that includes former Laker superstar Magic Johnson for the incredible sum of $2 billion, presumably because the new owners see massive untapped revenue potential in the Southern California market.

In this world, the logic of the Blue Jays being owned by Rogers, which also owns the stadium in which they play, is pretty obvious. The Jays provide their owner with guaranteed multimedia content, and the owner can transfer as much revenue to the team as is required to field a more-or-less competitive and interesting product. And in baseball, hope does indeed spring eternal.

In short, MLB operates much like a modern capitalist economy. The playing field is not level, but some revenue sharing within MLB allows smaller market teams to make money if they keep their player costs under control. Many teams are unlikely to ever win the World Series—just making the playoffs is a victory for them. But income transfers are used to soften the hard edges of the MLB free market for talent.

Team Sports at Major U.S. Universities— "Voluntary Servitude"

The team sports system at major U.S. universities is designed to ensure that everyone makes money—everyone, that is, except the athletes. Thanks to extensive TV coverage and related contracts for college football and basketball in particular, the top sports universities, their athletic departments, and the superstar coaches receive significant compensation. Annual salaries for U.S. college football and basketball coaches can reach into the millions of dollars.

But what about the athletes? The top ones usually receive an athletic scholarship, and a growing number are completing their degrees (although this is less common among the top basketball and football players). Moreover, the athletes are punished severely if they accept the smallest gift from an agent or supporter. Such a system has enormous potential for abuse and is in many ways little more than a form of voluntary servitude in which the uncompensated efforts of many young athletes generate significant incomes and wealth for a few.

Robber Barons: European Football as Unconstrained 19th-Century Capitalism

The last pro sports economic model we examine is European football (i.e., soccer), where almost anything goes. European football is comparable to the unconstrained capitalism of the 19th century, when enormous market power and wealth could be accumulated by a few wealthy individuals, sometimes called "robber barons," and everyone else was left to fend for themselves. Here's how it works.

First, European football has a long history, with each country having many clubs that are grouped into multiple divisions. Based on their play each season, the bottom two or three teams in each division are relegated (or sent down a division), and the top two or three teams in the lower divisions are promoted to replace them. The top few teams in the top division of each country are invited to play in annual pan-European tournaments, called the Champions League and the UEFA Europa League. Each country also has one or more single knockout tournament (such as the FA Cup in England, which involves every team in the English football association). As a result, all teams have multiple opportunities each year to win one or more championships.

Second, European football has access to a free and global market for player talent. Players are drawn from anywhere in the world. They sign contracts with individual clubs depending on what the market will bear, and their contract can be bought from, or sold to, other clubs. Players can also be lent to another club for a period of time. This free market for player talent drives up both player salaries and the cost of contract transfers for top players, and makes smaller and less-wealthy teams largely uncompetitive on the field. Upsets do happen on occasion, but the major tournaments and divisions are almost invariably won by a rich team with skilled and expensive players.

Third, there is limited revenue sharing within countries and across divisions. The operating conditions for revenue sharing vary by country. In Britain, teams in the top division, called the Premier League, generate and share more than a billion pounds of annual broadcast revenue. The estimated revenue gap between the richest and poorest clubs in the Premier League is about 1.7 times, which is smaller than the comparable gap in MLB (where it is at least four times). Staying in the top league is critically important for clubs—relegation means losing access to the rich TV dollars. In contrast, the two biggest clubs in Spain—Barcelona and Real Madrid—currently take half of the annual €600 million in football TV revenue in Spain, leaving the balance to be split among the remaining 18 clubs in the Spanish top division.[1] It is no surprise that Barcelona and Real Madrid invariably lead the way in Spain and in Europe, since they have the means to buy the very best players.

> European football has a long history, with each country having many clubs that are grouped into multiple divisions.

Fourth, some very rich individuals from around the world have been lured by the prestige of owning a European football club—as a very expensive "plaything" or because of the potential to achieve capital gains if the club's value rises. Football clubs in England have been particularly subject to purchase by rich foreigners—sometimes with success, but sometimes with disastrous results.

The result of this free market system? There are a few very rich football clubs—such as Manchester United and Chelsea FC in England, Barcelona and Real Madrid in Spain, and Bayern Munich in Germany—that are almost always competitive. Supporters of these clubs can reasonably expect their team to win championships each year. And there are upstart clubs where new owners come in with lots of money—clubs like Manchester City, which has bought some of the best players available and pushed into the top tier of European football, supported by a billionaire owner who is prepared to sustain massive financial losses (a loss of £97 million in 2012, which is actually down from £197 million in 2011) in order to achieve competitive success.

---

1   Iain Rogers, "Barcelona Against Sharing TV Revenue," *The Independent*, October 21, 2011.

In the next tier, there are many good—but not top-level—clubs (such as Everton and West Ham in England), which can move up and down between divisions depending on their results over the season. Their fans have to be satisfied with doing well in national tournaments, such as the FA Cup, and moving up a division if possible, or at least avoiding relegation.

European football is a modern-day example of 19th century capitalism, where the strong thrive and become ever more powerful, the majority manage to just get by, and the weak are left behind.

Below these clubs are many others that simply do not have the financial means to buy better players and compete at higher levels. They have to be content with developing the occasional star player who can later be sold, and with competing a division or two below the top clubs.

And then there are the outright financial disasters—clubs that have tried to compete with the big clubs, only to blow their budget and end up in financial turmoil. Storied British clubs such as Leeds United, Portsmouth FC, and Glasgow Rangers have all ended up in what is called "administration." Unable to pay their bills, they get taken over by a court-appointed administrator, are forced to sell star players to cover costs, and are usually docked points in the divisional standings as punishment for their financial mismanagement, which leads to their being relegated to a lower division.

In 2009, UEFA (Union of European Football Associations) moved to stem the mounting losses of some clubs. That year, the Financial Fair Play (FFP) regulations, which essentially amount to a flexible spending cap for clubs, were approved. Under FFP (which took effect in 2011), clubs can spend as much as they want, but revenues must cover their spending. If a club can generate more revenue, it can spend more on players. Teams must abide by FFP if they are to take part in European competitions, and violators face exclusion beginning in 2014–15. Individual nations are also taking action to reduce financial losses. The British Premier League, under pressure from the government, introduced a rule that clubs can sustain losses of no more than £105 million over the three seasons from 2013–14 to 2015–16. Failure to live within these bounds will result in points deducted from the standings.

FFP, along with other measures, should make European football more business-sustainable. But since there is no effort to level the playing field in terms of revenue sharing or controlling player costs, these measures will have only a limited impact on the competitiveness on the pitch. In short, European football today is a modern-day example of 19th century capitalism, where the strong thrive and become ever more powerful, the majority manage to just get by, and the weak are left behind. Just as it is somewhat of a contradiction that the "socialist" NFL is the top sport in the firmly capitalist U.S., it is ironic to find the unconstrained capitalism of European football on a continent with such a highly developed social welfare system.

Conclusion

Looking at pro sports leagues and teams as economic systems, it is the NFL that is the most collectivist, sharing 80 per cent of league revenues and having a player salary cap firmly in place. It has the most level playing field for its teams and fans when it comes to competitive conditions. And it is also the league with the most sustained financial success. The NHL is a mixed economy, with a salary cap to limit player costs and some sharing of revenues among franchises if and when required to protect franchise values.

Competitive conditions in the NBA are becoming more similar to those of the NHL. The NBA has a soft salary cap and has just begun enhanced revenue sharing, but it still has some teams that consistently dominate and some that chronically struggle financially. MLB's system is consistent with modern capitalism, with enough income transfers to allow most teams to make money and thus soften the hard edges of the free market, but with many teams unable to seriously contend for a World Series championship. And European football is the pro sport that operates like old-fashioned capitalism—with the robber barons firmly in charge.

Chapter 14

The NHL Business Environment: Four Detailed Examinations

Despite the 2012–13 lockout and the lowering of the salary cap, the NHL business model is still not fully stable. Interest in NHL hockey is regional, not spread evenly across North America ... and certainly not in the southern United States.

This chapter provides four case studies that examine in detail some different aspects of the NHL as a pro sports business.

Case One: The NHL Business Model Is Still Not Stable

The NHL survived the 2012–13 lockout, which was precipitated in order to get a new deal with the players. The players' share of revenues will decline in the 2014–15 season after two transitional years in which the salary cap was set as part of the negotiations. The many serious hockey fans across Canada and the northern United States are excited about the return of the fastest game on ice, while sports fans further south are less so. And that's the problem.

Demand for NHL hockey is regional, not spread evenly across North America. The NHL ventured into too many non-traditional markets in the southern U.S. in the hope of growing the game (and making more money from it), but the public there does not have the same passion for hockey. There was little passion for NHL hockey in the southern markets before the lockout, and there is little sign that anything has changed since the lockout ended. The NHL's business model is still broken, even after the four-month lockout in 2012–13 and the collective compensation rollback for the players.

What is the NHL business model? It is not a single, unitary business offering essentially the same product to all consumers and allowing all revenues and costs to be centrally controlled. Rather, it is a franchise model where individual owners acquire the right to be part of the league and to operate an NHL team in a specific location. Each time a new franchise is added, the existing franchises share the expansion fee, hence their interest in growing the game in non-traditional markets with large populations in the South.

The league tries to ensure "product quality" by having a common entry draft that makes the same young player talent pool available to all franchises. But players have the right to become free agents in the later stages of their careers, and this tends to erode the level playing field for talent.

The league also tries to create a more financially level playing field among the franchises in two ways. First, the NHL limits the share of "hockey-related revenues" that goes to the players. The 2013 agreement between players and owners saw the players' share fall from 57 per cent to 50 per cent in 2014–15, a level similar to that found in many other pro sports leagues.

Second, the NHL has a limited version of revenue sharing among the franchises. Revenue sharing is the one remaining area where the league could act more aggressively in order to support the existing weaker franchises. The problem with expanded revenue sharing, however, is that the NHL has a very limited pool of collective revenues from national TV coverage that could be shared. The NHL receives national TV revenues of about $600 million annually. Compare that with the $5 billion received annually by the National Football League.

CBS, NBC, FOX, and ESPN have agreed to pay a combined total of US$39.6 billion to broadcast all NFL games from 2014 to 2022 inclusively.

More aggressive NHL revenue sharing requires the richer teams—the Leafs, Rangers, Habs, Flyers, Canucks, Red Wings, and perhaps a few others—to dip into their pockets and transfer some of their own directly earned revenues to their poorer cousins, something they are understandably reluctant to do beyond some minimal amount.

Therefore, within the framework of the 2013 compensation agreement between owners and players, the success of each NHL franchise is determined fundamentally by the demand for hockey in each local market. If demand is solid, franchises succeed. But if consumers are generally uninterested in buying the product, no amount of wage cuts for the key employees—the players—is going to make these businesses successful.

So did the fans get a good deal out of the lockout and the resulting agreement? As expected, the 2012 negotiations between the NHL owners and the players association dragged on through the summer and fall and into the winter, before reaching a successful conclusion in January—just in time to save part of the 2013 season. It is impossible to tell the true status of any labour negotiation from the outside, but it was pretty obvious that there was a significant gap between the two sides. The owners expected a sharp rollback in the share of revenues going to the players—and that is what they eventually got. And while the players tried unsuccessfully to maintain the salary cap at 57 per cent of revenues, they put much more weight on getting the league to enhance revenue sharing among the franchises, which they did get—at least to some degree.

But rather than looking at the negotiations in terms of a win-lose battle between the owners and players, let's take the perspective of the fans of NHL hockey. Was this the best deal for them?

First, and most importantly, fans wanted a deal to get done in time for the NHL season to start as scheduled in early October 2012. That did not happen. The league had headed into the off-season with positive momentum from the spring 2012 playoffs, which saw a surprise winner in the Los Angeles Kings. The delay in starting the 2012 season broke the momentum and led many fans to question their commitment to NHL hockey, at least temporarily. That said, once the game came back in January 2013, so did the fans—to everyone's relief.

Second, most fans want a level playing field (or ice surface) in terms of competition, one that allows them to reasonably expect their team to make the playoffs regularly. But to have a more level ice surface in terms of competition, the league needed to create a more level surface financially. The introduction of a player salary cap in 2005 helped to create better financial conditions by making operating costs more equal, hence increasing the likelihood that a team like Phoenix could reach the conference finals (as the Coyotes, in fact, did in 2012). But despite the salary cap, by the end of the collective bargaining agreement's term following the 2011–12 season, there were still wide disparities in the ability of teams to generate revenues, and therefore in their ability to spend to the limit of the salary cap and to compete for the best free agents.

According to Forbes, the top eight NHL franchises (Toronto, New York Rangers, Montréal, Detroit, Boston, Chicago, Vancouver, and Philadelphia) had a market value in excess of $4 billion in 2012. Collectively, they made around $300 million in profits in 2011–12. Nine other teams made money, but 13 lost money, according to Forbes— over $20 million in the case of Phoenix. While the Forbes profitability numbers may not be precise to the last cent, they provide a good ballpark estimate of the financial positions of many teams. Therefore, it is fair to conclude that there are sharp differences among the teams in revenue-generation capacity and in their bottom line.

To us, this looks like a solid prima facie case for more revenue sharing among the teams, regardless where the salary cap is set. More revenue sharing would serve the interests of the fans by creating better long-term competitive and operating conditions for the league and its teams. Fans care about the end result—a competitive league in which their team could make the playoffs and compete for the Stanley Cup—and they don't care that much about the specific action to achieve this. During the course of the 2012–13 negotiations, NHL owners accepted the need for some enhancements to the league's revenue-sharing mechanism that would make it easier for the bottom teams to sustain a competitive player payroll above the salary cap floor. So the fans did make gains here.

Finally, the fans wanted a deal with a longer life, one that would avoid the threat of another lockout or strike for as long as possible. The players initially proposed a three-year deal. But to keep the fans happy and win their support, a longer deal was needed—and an eight-year deal is what the fans got.

Is it naive to think the fans' interests were ever factored into the negotiations? Probably. This was a battle between millionaire players and multi-millionaire, or even billionaire, owners. They may have paid lip service to the fans and to doing the right thing for the game when they addressed the media, but at the end of the day the issue was how to divide up the pie, both between the players and the owners and among the franchises. If the teams or the players had thought about the fans for just a moment, they might have reached a deal that made sense for all long before nearly half the 2012–13 season was lost.

Going forward, it appears that the NHL did not significantly hurt its brand with existing consumers of hockey by locking out the players for those four months. Average game attendance was up by 2.6 per cent (pro-rated for the shortened 2013 season). The fans quickly flocked back to the arenas in northern NHL markets where passion for hockey burns bright. Attendance numbers also were good in southern NHL markets, such as Nashville, Florida, Dallas, and Phoenix, perhaps because there was pent-up demand among existing fans and fewer games to attend in a shortened season.

Still, the fundamental issue remains: Can the NHL expand its fan base in markets where there is no culture of hockey? We remain skeptical. In our view, the only way to "fix" the broken NHL business model is by moving franchises to other locations where hockey is truly valued, since the costs of contraction, mainly in the form of having to repay expansion fees, is just too high for the other owners. If there is a bright spot on the horizon it is that Québec City should not have to wait forever. It is just a matter of time before common sense prevails, an owner (or the league collectively) gets tired of writing cheques, and a southern NHL franchise lands in the beautiful new building in Québec City.

Case Two: Who Were the Losers and Winners From the NHL Lockout?

The lockout lasted four months, with up to $1 billion in possible revenue forgone by the industry as the parties squabbled about the transition from one revenue-sharing system to another. So who are the biggest losers? And was anyone a winner?

To begin, and perhaps surprisingly, the lockout had limited negative impact on overall GDP in Canada, the U.S., and most of the cities and regions hosting NHL franchises. Here, it is important to separate the immediate financial impacts from the larger economic impacts. No doubt, there were financial losses caused by the lockout for the league and its stakeholders (the owners and their franchises, the players, and the leagues' various suppliers). But there was not much of an impact on the economy as a whole.

Why? Because the money that would have been spent by consumers on NHL games, either directly via ticket purchases or indirectly through the purchase of related services, was largely re-directed to other forms of consumption in the economy. There are always some "leakages" from this reallocation—like season-ticket holders who didn't seek a return of their payments already made. But, overall, for every financial loser, there was likely a winner that experienced increased sales as consumers redirected their purchasing power away from the NHL and its suppliers during the lockout.

So beyond the fans, who suffered from the lack of top-notch hockey? Who were the financial losers? First up are the players, who gave up 32 per cent of their pay when the 2012–13 NHL season was cut from 82 games to 48. The more a player was scheduled to make, the more he lost, with no guarantee of ever making it up. Some older players without contracts were never re-signed, as they were displaced after the lockout by younger and cheaper talent, so they are permanent losers. And after a 2013–14 transition year in which the team salary cap is reduced to $64.3 million (from a pro-rated $70.2 million the previous season), the players will have to live with a 50-50 split in NHL hockey-related revenues beginning in 2014–15, which will mean a lower cap over the near term at least.

Owners of profitable franchises were the next set of losers. This group includes all of the Canadian NHL teams, according to NHL business data produced by Forbes. The Leafs, Habs, and Canucks are the Canadian teams that make the largest profits, and were therefore the biggest losers in Canada last year. They and the other Canadian teams will have a chance to make this money back in future years under the new 50-50 revenue-sharing formula that favours the owners, since demand for tickets in these markets exceeds the available supply.

For the NHL franchises that lose money (up to half, according to the Forbes numbers), the 2012–13 lockout might actually have reduced their losses last season and could allow them to operate profitably down the road. They would thus become winners from the lockout— which was the point of the exercise. However, that result is subject to two important conditions: the rollback in the players' share of revenues to 50 per cent proves sufficient to bring these teams' operating costs into line with potential revenues; and their ticket-buying fans, corporate supporters, and advertisers continue to support the team. Average attendance went up slightly after the lockout, but we expect that some NHL franchises will continue to struggle financially.

Mass media that broadcast games, led by TSN, RDS, CBC, and NBC, were also financial losers, since they did not get the additional advertising revenue from NHL games they would have received when compared with their replacement programming. (In some cases, however, there were make-whole clauses in their contracts with the NHL and its teams, which required the league to supply an equivalent number of games at the current contract price to replace those that were lost. For NBC, this means its new contract with the league— which jumped from $200 million annually to $350 million in 2012–13— will be extended. And given that the NHL expects its next contract with NBC or one of its rivals to be bigger still, the shortened season delays the arrival of that larger future TV contract, thereby also costing the league and its owners more in lost revenue.

Then there are all the league's suppliers of labour and services: the team and league employees, including game officials; the staff in the arenas, restaurants, and bars frequented by fans; air services, hotels, and restaurants used by teams for away games; parking and other ground transportation to the game; suppliers of team sweaters and caps, etc. Again, few of these suppliers will ever fully replace the income lost.

Finally, as noted earlier, there are some winners—the many businesses that captured the reallocated spending by consumers. Various forms of entertainment likely saw a bump in 2012–13 revenue, including other hockey leagues, such as the American Hockey League and the junior leagues. There also may have been broader impacts on society, since NHL fans had more discretionary leisure time to spend on other activities.

Overall, the GDP impact of the NHL lockout was not significant. Many consumers of hockey simply shifted their discretionary leisure dollars and time away from NHL hockey and spent it elsewhere. But like so many other industrial relations disputes, almost everyone connected to the NHL was a net financial loser in the near term, and many will likely never make up the loss.

Case Three: The Cruel Economics of NHL Headshots and Enforcers

With every NHL season, there is more sad news about players who will never play again. In 2011, tragedy struck three times. Wade Belak tragically joined Rick Rypien and Derek Boogaard as NHL enforcers (or designated fighters) who died far too young. One is a tragedy, two is a sad coincidence, three is a trend. Enforcer George Parros was the latest victim of a severe concussion during a fight in the first game of the 2013–14 season, rekindling debate about the role and long-term impact of fighting in the modern game.

Moreover, a number of star players have been forced to quit the game prematurely. Marc Savard, Eric Lindros, and Paul Kariya were all forced to retire early due to severe head trauma and recurring concussion symptoms. Even the best player in the NHL today, Sidney Crosby, has had to take significant stretches away from the game to recover from blows to the head. And after two or more concussions, Crosby may be only one more headshot away from retirement.

Sadly, there is a cruel economic perspective on these tragedies, one that might offer some clues as to why fighting and headshots are still tolerated in the NHL.

From the perspective of the league and teams, there is little doubt that aggressive play sells tickets to NHL games—indeed, aggressive physical play is integral to the NHL's brand. Just look at the excited reaction of fans when a fight breaks out. The same cannot be said about headshots, which are abhorred almost universally. But the fact that the league has not removed headshots from the game entirely says a great deal about what the NHL is selling—physical play, as much as goals and great saves.

There is also scant evidence that concussions to star players, or serious risks to fighters, detract from league or team revenues. Excessive violence may be a factor in the NHL's low national media revenues in the U.S., but we have seen little hard evidence that violence is bad for the business of pro hockey—on the contrary, the rise of new sports like mixed martial arts reinforces the evidence that restrained violence sells in our society.

On the expense side of the ledger, however, teams buy insurance and pay premiums on player contracts, against the risk that a serious injury will prevent a player from playing for a long duration. If concussions keep mounting in the NHL and insurance claims have to be paid out, teams will have to pay higher premiums eventually, adding to team costs and eating into their profits.

An additional economic factor could force the NHL to reconsider the level of physical play that is tolerated in the league. Former and current players in the National Football League recently banded together to bring a lawsuit against the NFL and its owners, contending that the league concealed the impact of head trauma on players and did little to stop concussions from occurring. In September 2013, the NFL reached a $765-million, out-of-court settlement with the NFL Players Association to prevent a lawsuit from proceeding, although this amount is under judicial review and could increase. These funds are to be used by players past and present to help deal with the post-career impact of concussions. The NFL has also progressively tightened the rules with respect to head contact, even banning coaches from the New Orleans Saints for a year for offering bounties for violent hits.

The threat of rising insurance premiums and the risk of a future lawsuit by the players are the most likely financial brakes on headshots in the NHL. These economic threats could force the league, teams, and players association to develop and pay for more extensive programs to deal with the physical and mental health issues facing current and former players.

For the players, the allure of an NHL paycheque and the associated status is enormous. Some players can only make it to, and stay in, the NHL by becoming fighters, so it becomes a matter of how much personal risk and punishment they are willing to absorb in order to earn an NHL spot. While a few fighters have had their careers ended in a fight, for many, the risk seems worth taking. However, the players may not adequately factor in the risks of emotional and physical pain from endless hockey fights, and the danger of painkilling drugs, especially mixed with alcohol.

Headshots and resulting concussions are another matter, since they are generally random acts and hard to factor into a player's risk–reward estimations. Certainly the risk of concussion or other serious injury should be an incentive for players to sign a long-term contract if possible, in the event that they are severely injured and unable to play for an extended period of time. But even though many players have been pushed out of hockey by cerebral concussions, no one thinks it will happen to them—just like smokers never think they'll be the one to get lung cancer.

Will economic factors bring these dangerous practices to an end? There is little evidence so far that there is a severe impact on revenues from concussions to star players, and insurance costs to teams are probably still low enough to be absorbed. Fighting, even when it is staged between designated enforcers, probably does sell tickets. So what would it take to change? Headshots and fighting could be curtailed if the league was willing to take more forceful action to suspend and otherwise punish the aggressors.

If a superstar like Sidney Crosby were to have to end his career early due to concussions, that could get the NHL's attention. The NFL has figured out that quarterbacks are a major draw for fans, and the rules have been changed accordingly to offer them extra protection. But given the NHL's history, it could take something as terrible as an on-ice fatality as a result of a fight or a violent blow to the head to be the catalyst for major change. Bill Masterton's death during a NHL game in 1968 helped make helmets more common, although it still took more than a decade before the rule making helmets mandatory would be grandfathered in. Similarly, it took decades—and the partial loss of vision by more than one NHL player—for visors to become compulsory for new players. But, as discussed earlier, a successful class action lawsuit by former players against the league for ignoring evidence of long-term impairment from head trauma or fighting would provide a strong financial incentive to change.

For now, exceptional violence, in the form of staged fights and random headshots, remains part of the NHL game and economic model, and punishment of the aggressors by the league is inconsistent and often seemingly arbitrary. The consequences for some players and their families can be tragic.

Case Four: Why Are the Coyotes Still in Arizona?

A deal was patched together in the spring of 2013 to "save" the renamed Arizona (formerly the Phoenix) Coyotes. The National Hockey League franchise has been preserved by the combination of new owners and a large de facto operating subsidy ($15 million annually, minus certain arena revenues) from the city of Glendale, a suburb of Phoenix and the owner of the Coyotes' home arena.

How long the deal will last is an open question—the current arrangement is guaranteed for five years. But in the meantime, the NHL avoids having to move the franchise—and could therefore earn some healthy expansion fees in hockey-ready markets such as Québec City. Meanwhile, others carry the risk and costs of operating a hockey team in the desert.

This deal does two good things for the NHL. First, it allows the league to shed the risks and costs of operating the team. The new owners, most of whom are Canadian, apparently believe they can turn things around in the Phoenix area—or at least minimize the franchise's losses until they are allowed to move it elsewhere. They have agreed to operate the team in Glendale for at least five years. So this deal provides an element of stability for the NHL and prevents the franchise from moving to another more hockey-hungry market for now.

For its part, the Glendale city council agreed, by a vote of 4 to 3, to throw more good money after bad (not a practice that is recommended in economics) and provide an operating subsidy to the franchise in the form of an arena management services agreement. In so doing, they are trying to protect their investment in the arena, which lies on the western edge of the Phoenix area, was built with local taxpayer money, and was supposed to draw other investment and spending activity to Glendale.

We have attended Coyotes games at that arena. While the building is an attractive and modern place to watch an NHL game, we could see only limited evidence that Glendale's strategy for attracting investment has worked, even with the Arizona Cardinals' impressive NFL stadium next door. Without a pro sports franchise as a tenant, the Glendale arena and its neighbouring hotel, mall, and entertainment facilities would risk becoming stranded assets—a modern Western ghost town. So the Glendale council was damned if they did, damned if they didn't. In the end, they did, and the NHL benefited.

Second, and more importantly, keeping the Coyotes in Glendale/ Phoenix preserves the NHL's ability to earn significant expansion fees by locating new franchises in hockey-hungry markets, such as Québec City, Markham, and perhaps Seattle or Kansas City.

Some might label this strategy as cynical; others would call it just good business (especially with local taxpayers underwriting part of the risk). Even divided into 30 parts, an expansion fee of $250 million or more per franchise would be attractive to the NHL's current members.

Still, this patched-together deal cannot fix the underlying economics of hockey in the desert. The Phoenix area is not a natural location for an NHL franchise, despite its large population. There is no evident hockey culture; the climate is warm in winter and scorching hot in summer. The Phoenix sports market is cluttered and probably saturated. Glendale is on the wrong side of town, away from the upscale Scottsdale and Tempe suburbs with their higher purchasing power. Phoenix itself is not a wealthy market. And getting to Coyotes' games in rush-hour traffic is frustrating and time-consuming. None of these things can be fixed by a new owner and a creative subsidy from Glendale.

The Coyotes' deal is good for the NHL and the team's occasional local fans, bad for Glendale taxpayers, and uncertain for the new ownership group. And it likely also means that fans in Québec City will have to wait a bit longer for their own team.

Chapter 15
What Will the Canadian Pro Sports Scene Look Like in 2035?

Today, baseball, football, soccer, and (most of all) hockey draw huge numbers of fans to stadiums and to television screens across the country. But what will the professional sports scene look like in the future?

Professional sports are about giving the fans what they want today, while at the same time preparing for the future. But what will that future look like? In this chapter, we draw on our economic forecasting skills (since we are, after all, economists) and combine them with the analytical framework developed throughout this book to define what the Canadian professional sports scene could look like nearly a quarter of a century from now—in 2035.

The professional sports scene could, and likely will, change significantly over the next 20-plus years. A quarter of a century ago, boxing and horse racing were mainstream sports. Professional mixed martial arts (MMA) fighting did not exist. And soccer was still a marginal sport in North America. Look at how much things have changed since then. The work presented here is based mainly on an extrapolation of what exists today—it does not attempt to predict everything that could happen in the professional sports world in North

America in the coming years. However, it does include the impact of population aging and the continued rise in immigration on the professional sports scene in Canada.

Looking Ahead Based on the Four Pillars

Throughout this book, we have frequently referred back to the four market pillars for professional sports franchise success, which we first introduced in Chapter 2. Those four market pillars are:

- market size;
- income levels;
- a strong corporate presence;
- a level playing field.

To paint a picture of what the professional sports scene will look like in Canada in the future, we looked at how each of the four pillars is likely to evolve in Canada over the coming years. We decided to take the long view, looking at how things will change between now and 2035. Fortunately, we were able to use The Conference Board of Canada's long-term economic forecast for Canada and for each province as a basis.

The Board's long-term economic forecast has been produced for over two decades and provides a strong foundation for our work here.

Market Size

This first pillar, market size, is key to determining a local market's professional sports capacity. In 2010 (which we will use as our baseline year), Canada contained six census metropolitan areas (CMAs) with populations greater than 1 million—Toronto, Montréal, Vancouver, Calgary, Ottawa–Gatineau, and Edmonton. (See Table 12.) By 2035, we project there will be one more: Winnipeg. All seven of these CMAs are currently home to a National Hockey League franchise. Hamilton and Québec City (contenders to obtain NHL franchises, according to our analysis in Chapter 12) will both see their populations rise above 900,000, but neither is expected to reach the 1 million threshold by 2035. Therefore, there were nine CMAs with populations of 750,000 or greater in 2010, and there will still be nine in 2035.

Table 12
Population Growth in Canada's CMAs

CMA	Population in 2010 (000s)	Population in 2035 (000s)	Change	Average annual percentage change
Toronto	5741.4	8995.1	3253.7	1.8
Montréal	3859.3	4926.5	1067.2	1.0
Vancouver	2391.3	3588.8	1197.5	1.6
Calgary	1242.6	2063.9	821.3	2.1
Ottawa	1239.1	1704.5	465.4	1.3
Edmonton	1176.3	1703.3	527.0	1.5
Winnipeg	753.6	1094.2	340.6	1.5
Hamilton	740.2	943.8	203.6	1.0
Québec City	754.4	919.2	164.8	0.8
KWC	492.4	706.4	214.0	1.5
London	492.2	602.5	110.3	0.8
Oshawa	364.2	560.4	196.2	1.7
Halifax	403.2	498.1	94.9	0.8
Victoria	358.1	474.2	116.1	1.1
St. Catharines	404.4	440.3	35.9	0.3
Saskatoon	265.3	430.2	164.9	2.0
Windsor	330.9	375.3	44.4	0.5
Regina	215.1	305.3	90.1	1.4
Sherbrooke	197.3	255.8	58.5	1.0
Abbotsford	174.3	249.2	74.9	1.4
St. John's	192.3	224.9	32.6	0.6
Kingston	162.5	191.1	28.5	0.6
Moncton	126.4	178.8	52.3	1.4
Sudbury	164.7	168.4	3.7	0.1
Trois-Rivières	146.5	159.9	13.4	0.4
Saguenay	152.2	137.1	−15.1	−0.4
Saint John	128.0	130.0	2.0	0.1
Thunder Bay	126.7	116.4	−10.3	−0.3

Sources: Statistics Canada; The Conference Board of Canada

Between 2010 and 2035, Toronto is expected to post the largest population increase of any Canadian CMA—up by more than 3 million, to almost 9 million inhabitants. Vancouver and Montréal are next, with the population of each anticipated to increase by more than 1 million. Overall, fourteen Canadian CMAs are forecast to achieve a population increase of more than 100,000 during that period.

Table 13 provides another demographic dimension—that of population aging. While most of Canada's CMAs will witness a population increase (thereby increasing their professional sports market capacity), the share of their populations aged 65 and over will increase rapidly over the next 25 years.[1] In Toronto, the population aged 65 and over will increase by more than 1 million, equal to one-third of the expected population increase. And this pattern is even more pronounced in Vancouver and Montréal. In Vancouver, the population aged 65 and over will be equivalent to one-half of the overall population increase. In Montréal, that figure rises to two-thirds. So while 14 CMAs will see their populations increase by 100,000 or more between 2010 and 2035, only 10 will see their under-65 population increase by 100,000 or more. As a glance at the crowd at almost any major sporting event today clearly shows, the core market for professional sports is people well under the age of 65. Therefore, population aging in Canada will have a mild dampening effect on the overall growth of the pro sports market.

---

1   While those aged 65 and older will continue to attend sports events, they are likely to do so less frequently than younger members of the population. Therefore, this demographic change must be taken into account when looking at a market's capacity to support professional sports franchises.

Table 13
Canadian CMAs Face Aging Populations

CMA	Share of 65+ in 2006 (%)	Population aged less than 65 in 2010 (000s)	Share of 65+ in 2035 (%)	Population aged less than 65 in 2035 (000s)	Change in population less than 65 (000s)	Average annual per cent change (%)
Toronto	12	5052.4	22	7016.2	1963.7	1.3
Montréal	14	3319	25	3694.9	375.9	0.4
Vancouver	13	2080.4	25	2691.6	611.2	1.0
Calgary	9	1130.8	18	1692.4	561.6	1.6
Ottawa	12	1090.4	22	1329.5	239.1	0.8
Edmonton	11	1046.9	20	1362.6	315.7	1.1
Winnipeg	14	648.1	19	884.1	236.1	1.3
Hamilton	15	629.2	25	707.8	78.6	0.5
Québec City	14	648.7	25	689.4	40.6	0.2
KWC	12	433.3	22	551	117.7	1.0
London	14	423.3	24	457.9	34.6	0.3
Oshawa	11	324.1	21	442.7	118.6	1.3
Halifax	12	354.8	27	364.6	9.8	0.1
Victoria	18	293.6	30	331.9	38.3	0.5
St. Catharines	18	331.6	28	317	−14.6	−0.2
Saskatoon	12	233.4	17	357	123.6	1.7
Windsor	13	287.8	23	289	1.1	0.0

(continued ...)

Table 13 (cont'd)
Canadian CMAs Face Aging Populations

CMA	Share of 65+ in 2006 (%)	Population aged less than 65 in 2010 (000s)	Share of 65+ in 2035 (%)	Population aged less than 65 in 2035 (000s)	Change in population less than 65 (000s)	Average annual per cent change (%)
Regina	13	187.2	18	250.3	63.1	1.2
Sherbrooke	14	169.7	25	191.9	22.2	0.5
Abbotsford	13	151.6	25	186.9	35.3	0.8
St. John's	11	171.2	30	157.9	–13.3	–0.3
Kingston	15	138.2	25	143.3	5.2	0.1
Moncton	14	108.7	30	125	16.2	0.6
Sudbury	15	140	25	126.3	–13.7	–0.4
Trois-Rivières	17	121.6	28	115.1	–6.5	–0.2
Saguenay	15	129.3	26	101.4	–27.9	–1.0
Saint John	14	110.1	30	90.9	–19.2	–0.8
Thunder Bay	16	106.4	26	86.2	–20.3	–0.8

Sources: Statistics Canada; The Conference Board of Canada.

Income Levels

Over the next 25 years, the Conference Board forecasts that economic growth in Canada will slow to less than 2 per cent annually, due largely to population aging and slower labour force growth. Only two provinces—Alberta and Saskatchewan—will grow faster than the national average, as they continue to benefit from strong demand for commodities from emerging countries, such as India and China.

This growth outlook bodes well for the relative wealth of markets such as Calgary, Edmonton, Regina, and Saskatoon. Well-managed pro sports teams in these markets can reasonably expect to have financial success. Toronto is Canada's largest pro sports market, and we expect wealth to continue to grow in the Greater Toronto Area. The region will continue to benefit from a large influx of immigrants, boosting the area's domestic demand and overall economic activity.

Table 14
GDP growth, 2010–35
(GDP, 2002 $ millions)

Province	GDP in 2010 (2002 $ millions)	GDP in 2035 (2002 $ millions)	Average annual per cent change (%)
Newfoundland and Labrador	17,643	21,325	0.8
Prince Edward Island	3,829	5,658	1.6
Nova Scotia	27,046	36,564	1.2
New Brunswick	21,891	29,474	1.2
Quebec	253,413	382,348	1.7
Ontario	485,010	835,343	1.9
Manitoba	39,577	67,238	2.1
Saskatchewan	39,438	70,862	2.4
Alberta	178,345	345,160	2.7
British Colombia	153,971	250,906	2.0
Canada	1,234,524	2,067,172	2.1

Sources: Statistics Canada; The Conference Board of Canada.

A Strong Corporate Presence

The paradigm linking people to jobs has shifted somewhat—from "people go where the jobs are" to "companies go where the people are." Today, companies want to be based where they can be confident they will find the skilled labour they need over the short, medium, and long term.[2] Accordingly, we expect that the number of corporate head offices will increase more rapidly in areas where the population will be increasing at a faster pace, particularly in those areas with a relatively younger population. Table 13 shows that growth in the under-65 population will be stronger in Toronto, Vancouver, Calgary, Edmonton, Regina, Saskatoon, Kitchener–Waterloo–Cambridge, Oshawa, and Winnipeg. Accordingly, we expect that these markets are likely to post the strongest increase in the number of head offices moving forward. In the case of Toronto, Calgary, and Vancouver, this will be the continuation of a well-established trend. For Edmonton, Regina, Saskatoon, Kitchener–Waterloo–Cambridge, Oshawa, and Winnipeg, this expected expansion of head offices will improve their financial capacity to support pro sports.

A Level Playing Field

The value of the Canadian dollar versus the U.S. greenback is a critical element in the business success of Canadian pro sports franchises in the National Hockey League and Major League Baseball, as they have to compete against teams based in the United States. Because player salaries in these leagues are set in U.S. dollars, a strong loonie reduces the Canadian-dollar cost of player salaries, while a weak loonie increases those costs. The Conference Board's expectation is that the dollar will remain relatively healthy in relation to the U.S. dollar over the longer term.

---

2   See The Conference Board of Canada, *City Magnets: Benchmarking the Attractiveness of Canada's CMAs* (Ottawa: The Conference Board of Canada, 2007).

Another plus for Canadian teams is the fact that Canada's fiscal position is much healthier than that of the United States. The U.S. federal government will eventually have to tackle its fiscal deficit, which has fallen to under $700 billion but will rise again due to pressure on social programs unless these are addressed structurally. U.S. states and cities will also have to deal with their structural fiscal imbalances. (Detroit filed for bankruptcy in August 2013.) To do so, U.S. jurisdictions will likely have to increase taxes eventually. As this happens, any gaps between Canadian and U.S. personal and business tax rates will diminish. This would be good news for Canadian franchises playing in North American professional sports leagues, as it would improve their relative competitive position.

Both of these factors suggest that, unlike in the past, Canadian franchises will have little financial incentive to leave Canada for greener pastures south of the border. The 2011 return of the Jets to Winnipeg is a reflection of the changed economic conditions in Canada and bodes well for pro sports on this side of the border over the next two decades.

Will professional sports leagues increase their efforts to level the playing field among their teams? We think Major League Baseball will. With people being offered a greater variety of sports and cultural activities from which to choose, we believe MLB will eventually have to come up with some type of system that will either limit the spread between the highest and lowest team payrolls and/or enrich the revenue-sharing scheme among franchises even further than it did in the 2011 bargaining agreement. MLB has already changed its playoff format to include one more team per league, starting in the 2012 season. And pressure to become more competitive may come not only from fans, but also from owners of franchises in smaller markets who are tired of not getting their fair share of the pie.

A Fearless Forecast: The Professional Sports Scene in Canada in 2035

Hockey

What does this all mean for the professional sports scene in Canada by 2035? In earlier chapters, we stated that an NHL franchise in Canada needed a minimum market of close to 800,000 to succeed. As shown in Table 12, there were nine CMAs with a population at or above that threshold in 2010, and there will still be just nine in 2035. Kitchener–Waterloo–Cambridge will come close to the threshold, with a population of a little over 700,000 by 2035, but only 550,000 of its residents will be under the age of 65.

We therefore forecast that there will be no more than nine NHL cities in Canada in 2035. This includes the markets with existing teams— Toronto, Montréal, Ottawa–Gatineau, Winnipeg, Calgary, Edmonton, and Vancouver—and two potential new markets—Québec City and Hamilton (recognizing that Hamilton will face major arena renovations and potential territorial fees if it is to succeed in acquiring a team).

Unfortunately for residents of the Maritimes, they will have to wait longer than 25 years to witness the appearance of NHL hockey in their region. Halifax, the Maritimes' largest city, will be home to just under 500,000 people in 2035. And out West, although Saskatoon will have grown to 430,000 in 2035, the city will still be too small to sustain an NHL franchise.

If the financial challenges of acquiring a franchise can be met, we foresee the introduction of NHL teams in Québec City and Hamilton, and a second team in the Toronto metropolitan area over the next 25 years.

For Toronto, Montréal, and Vancouver, the growth in their populations prompts the question of whether any could support a second NHL franchise. We see potential in only one of these markets—Toronto. By 2035, the population in the Toronto CMA will reach 9 million people, up more than 50 per cent from the current 5.7 million. And for the Greater Toronto Area as a whole, the head count will grow to 10.5 million from the current 6.8 million. While that population will be older on average that it is today, the under-65 population will still grow by 2 million. Corporate headquarters are likely to continue to increase in Toronto, providing additional potential support for a second NHL franchise in the Toronto CMA.

The challenge for a second Toronto franchise will be to make the business economics work, since the cost of entry into the NHL will be steep. Those costs include the cost of acquiring a franchise, building a quality playing facility (though Markham has debated the construction of a new facility), and addressing the Leafs' territorial rights. While it is difficult to put a final tally on the start-up costs, our estimates start at $750 million and increase up to $1 billion (in 2010 dollars) or more. There is also the potential issue of dealing with the new ownership structure for the Maple Leafs (under which media giants Bell and Rogers are co-owners of the franchise) and gaining access to broadcast media for games. However, if Bell and Rogers decide to work out an arrangement and are prepared to provide access to the media market, this could create the conditions for a second NHL franchise in the Toronto area.

Therefore, if the financial challenges of acquiring and operating a franchise successfully can be met, we foresee the introduction of NHL teams in Québec City and Hamilton, plus the addition of a second team in the Toronto CMA over the next 25 years.[3] These additions would increase the number of Canadian NHL teams to ten.

As a point of comparison, six new Canadian teams joined the NHL between 1970 and 1990. Vancouver was the first addition in 1970. Edmonton, Winnipeg, and Québec City were folded into the NHL following the dismantling of the World Hockey Association in 1979. The Flames arrived in Calgary from Atlanta in 1980, and Ottawa was awarded an expansion franchise that began play in the 1992–93 season. But the Québec City franchise left for Colorado in 1995, while Winnipeg's team left for Phoenix in 1996.

---

3   The plan to build a new NHL-scale arena in Markham increases the potential for a second NHL franchise in the Greater Toronto Area.

(Winnipeg regained its status as an NHL city in 2011 when Atlanta's second NHL franchise—the Thrashers—was relocated north to Canada.)

Baseball and Basketball

We do not foresee an additional NHL franchise in either Montréal or Vancouver over the next 25 years, but we believe there will be developments in the sports scenes of both markets. Montréal already possesses the basic market conditions required to support a MLB franchise and will strengthen its position over our forecast horizon. Therefore, it could be home to a MLB franchise for a second time. And Vancouver could be home to a National Basketball Association franchise, also for a second time.

> The NBA could return to Vancouver one day and be successful, especially if the Canadian dollar remains strong.

Looking at the Montréal market, the population of the Montréal CMA is projected to rise to almost 5 million by 2035, an increase of over 1 million. Two-thirds of that increase will be aged 65 and over—which is why we believe Montréal will be an even better market for baseball in the future. Baseball, with its more leisurely pace and quieter atmosphere that gives fans a chance to chat with fellow fans "over a cold one," is better suited to attracting an older fan base. But for Montréal to get its team back, Major League Baseball will have to create a more level playing field among its franchises. Without such an adjustment, which would give every team a chance to be more competitive and maintain fan interest over the long term, MLB will not return to Montréal—fans there will simply not support a team that has virtually no chance of ever winning a championship. And, of course, the return of MLB in Montréal would require a new stadium and deep-pocketed ownership.

Vancouver, like Montréal, is projected to see a population increase of over 1 million over the next 25 years, and it should attract more corporate headquarters. Most of the population increase will be due to immigration, much of which will come from Asia, where the popularity of basketball has grown rapidly.

Vancouver demonstrated its appetite for basketball with the Grizzlies, and that appetite should continue to grow. Although the Grizzlies left Vancouver following the 2000–01 season, the population of the Vancouver CMA at that time was barely 2 million and the Canadian dollar was sinking fast, on its way to a historic low. Those conditions have now changed. The NBA could return to Vancouver one day and be successful there, especially if the Canadian dollar remains strong. With a population of 3.5 million in 2035, the Vancouver market will be large enough to sustain franchises in the NHL, CFL, Major League Soccer, and the NBA—but not MLB.

Football

In Chapter 11, we identified six potential new markets for the CFL: Ottawa–Gatineau (where the league is already scheduled to return in 2014), London, Kitchener–Waterloo–Cambridge, Moncton, Halifax, and Québec City. While it may still be some time before any of these cities join the CFL, all will have the required market conditions to be successful in the league within the foreseeable future. The challenge will be to identify an owner, or better yet to create a local community ownership structure, that would provide a sustainable business model for a CFL team in these communities.

Pushing the analysis out to 2035 adds one more market to the list of potential CFL franchises—Saskatoon. Saskatoon will witness a rise in population from 265,000 in 2010 to 430,000 in 2035, thanks largely to its ability to attract international immigrants and migrants from elsewhere in Canada. What's more, the share of the city's population aged 65 and over will be among the lowest of any Canadian urban centre in 2035. Why will people move to Saskatoon? Commodity-fuelled economic growth will be relatively strong over the next 25 years, allowing for sustained job creation and a growth in corporate head offices. Indeed, we expect that Saskatchewan will post the fastest growth rate among Canada's provinces over the next

25 years. So, the province will eventually have both the population and the incomes required to support two CFL franchises. What a rivalry Saskatoon versus Regina would be!

> Given its growth rate and strong commodity-fuelled economy, Saskatchewan will eventually have the population and the incomes required to support two CFL franchises.

There is another possibility—a National Football League team in Toronto. The ramifications, of course, would be huge. There would be direct repercussions for the CFL's Argonauts and for the entire CFL, particularly for our projected new CFL teams in Kitchener–Waterloo–Cambridge and London. And the entire GTA sports scene would be affected. With an NFL team in Toronto, would there be room for a second NHL team in the city? While no concrete plan to bring the NFL to Toronto has been announced, the possibility of that happening between now and 2035 exists.

Soccer

In recent years, another sport has emerged as a major professional team sport in North America—soccer. Canada is now home to three Major League Soccer (MLS) teams: Toronto FC, Vancouver Whitecaps, and Montréal Impact. It is no coincidence that the teams are based in Canada's three largest and most diverse cities. On May 12, 2012, the latest addition, the Montréal Impact, played at home in front of nearly 61,000 fans—a record for Canadian professional soccer. Population diversity comes into play as an important factor in the rise of soccer's popularity, since most immigrants come from countries where soccer is the traditional favourite sport.

Looking ahead, soccer will continue to grow in Canada. Given their success so far in attracting fans, and given the growing Canadian interest in and media coverage of soccer, and the step-by-step growth model being used by MLS, we expect all three Canadian teams to continue as sustainable operations in the future. Moreover, Canada welcomes over 200,000 immigrants a year, a number that should grow as labour force conditions tighten due to an aging workforce, requiring employers to look outside Canada for talent. As a result, the share of the population born abroad will continue to rise, bringing more pro soccer fans to Canada.

The combination of a larger population and an expected continued rise in diversity provides the perfect mix for an expansion of Major League Soccer in Canada.

Will there be more MLS franchises in Canada by 2035? We think so. The population of Calgary is expected to surpass 2 million by 2035, and the populations of Edmonton and Ottawa are anticipated to climb to more than 1.7 million by 2035. Edmonton already has a pro soccer team in the North American Soccer League (NASL), Ottawa will acquire one in 2014, and these three cities already have diverse populations. In the 2011 Census, for example, the share of the foreign-born population stood at 28.5 per cent in Calgary— higher than Montréal's 24.3 per cent, which itself is higher than the national average share of 22 per cent. (In Edmonton, that share stood at 22.7 per cent, while it was 21 per cent in Ottawa.) So the combination of a larger population and an expected continued rise in diversity provides the perfect mix for an expansion of MLS in Canada. Edmonton, Calgary, and Ottawa could all be home to an MLS franchise by 2035. And with populations expected to exceed 2 million in Calgary and 1.7 million in Edmonton and Ottawa, we believe these three markets will be able to support NHL, CFL, and MLS franchises by 2035.

And what about cricket? Globally, cricket is second only to soccer in popularity. Twenty20—or T20—is a new version of cricket that was introduced in 2003. A T20 game lasts about two and half hours, about the same length as games in most other popular North American team sports. And T20 is huge now in Asia, Australia, England, and the Caribbean—countries and regions that are major sources of immigration to Canada. While the creation of a North American professional cricket league may seem like a stretch today, the continued arrival of 200,000 or more immigrants per year over the next 25 years will alter Canada's demographic picture significantly— and, in all likelihood, its professional sports scene as well.

Conclusion

The professional sports scene in Canada will continue to expand over the next 25 years. The conditions for growth are right—the Canadian dollar will likely remain relatively healthy and the taxation gap with the U.S. is expected to continue to narrow. This will allow existing franchises to prosper, and offer a better chance for new franchises to succeed. Canada could be home to 10 NHL teams, with new franchises in Québec City and Hamilton, and a second team in the Toronto CMA. If the league conditions are right and the city gets a new stadium, Montréal could once again be home to a Major League Baseball team. And with its continuing rise in population, Vancouver should be in a position to get a second chance at a National Basketball Association franchise.

As for the CFL, in Chapter 11 we identified six potential new markets in the near future. Looking ahead to 2035, one more market can be added to that list. Saskatoon will enjoy rapid economic and population growth and should see a rise in corporate presence, making it a suitable home for a new CFL franchise. The key will be to create an ownership structure that is right for the community.

Major League Soccer is on the rise. Canada is now home to three MLS teams and could support as many as six by 2035—Calgary, Edmonton, and Ottawa will all be sound options for MLS over the long term.

In short, the future is bright for pro sports in Canada. Given the continuing increase in the population and a Canadian dollar that should remain relatively healthy, there is no reason to expect any of the existing Canadian franchises in any of the major pro sports leagues to move south of the border over the next 25 years. And there are many reasons why we can expect the number of Canadian-based franchises to grow.

Chapter 16
Closing Thoughts

Professional sports are more than just entertainment in Canada—they are big businesses with revenues totalling at least $1.5 billion annually. Some pro sports franchises succeed, others don't. Is success or failure a matter of simple luck? Not at all— it's economics!

This book has demonstrated that basic economics matter fundamentally to the financial success of a professional sports franchise in a given market. Throughout the book, we have developed and used extensively an analytical framework that explains the success and failures of most professional franchises, not only in Canada but around the globe. Under our framework, there are four key pillars: market size, income levels, a sound corporate presence, and a level playing field. If these four market-based pillars are in place and are strong enough for a given franchise, they provide a strong foundation for the business success of a professional sports franchise over the long run.

We have also outlined three franchise-specific factors that are critical to success. They are: ownership and management, the home facility in which the franchise plays, and fan support. The market conditions (the four pillars) might be in place, but bad management, an inadequate facility, or insufficient fan support can all be detrimental to the business success of a franchise.

Of course, we recognize that there will likely always be some wealthy pro sports franchise owners for whom money is no object, and for whom losing a few million dollars a year is no cause for concern. But for the others—and they make up the majority—the market fundamentals and franchise-specific factors matter.

Using this framework, we were able to explain why the Québec Nordiques and Winnipeg Jets left Canada in the mid-1990s. But we also established that Canada could, today, support as many as nine NHL franchises, with Québec City and Hamilton having the proper market conditions to welcome teams. However, Winnipeg, Québec City, and Hamilton all remain markets that are at the lower limit of what is required to support an NHL team, so dedicated ownership will be key to the success of the new-born Jets and of potential new franchises in Québec City and Hamilton. By 2035, our analysis suggests, a second NHL team could see the light of day in Toronto, taking total NHL franchises in Canada to ten. But saturation of the Toronto pro sports market is a risk factor that will have to be managed.

We also used our framework to conclude that there is room for expansion in Canada by the Canadian Football League. If dedicated owners can be found and CFL-standard stadiums are prepared, our analysis indicates there could be up to 12 CFL teams within a decade from now, starting with the addition of Ottawa in 2014 and followed by Québec City, Halifax or Moncton, and London or Kitchener. Over the next 25 years, the league could grow to as many as 15 teams, with the potential for franchises in both Moncton and Halifax, as well as in both London and Kitchener, and a second franchise in Saskatchewan, based in Saskatoon.

As for Major League Baseball, Montréal already has the necessary market conditions in place to be home to a franchise. The city is large and wealthy enough, has a healthy corporate presence, and the stronger Canadian dollar is a key factor in its favour. But among the major professional leagues, MLB has the least-level playing field competitively, since it has no player salary cap. That reality, along with the lack of a quality baseball facility, reduces Montréal's appeal to prospective owners as a site for an MLB franchise. Still, we are not closing the door to the possibility of MLB returning to the city, particularly if a media conglomerate were to get involved; one that would broadcast Montréal baseball games in French and English.

Major League Soccer is on the rise. Canada is now home to three MLS teams and could support up to an three more by 2035—Calgary, Edmonton, and Ottawa will all be sound options for MLS over the long term. And with its continuing growth in population, Vancouver should be in a position to get a second chance at hosting a National Basketball Association franchise.

The bottom line? Professional sports is a lucrative business that is doing well in Canada. The analysis conducted throughout this book leads us to conclude that there is little likelihood of any Canadian team moving south of the border over the next 25 years. Au contraire! We see expansion prospects in Canada for the NHL, CFL, MLS, and NBA, and perhaps for MLB under changed league conditions. The Canadian dollar is far above the levels it fell to in the early 2000s and should stay relatively strong for the foreseeable future. The Canadian economy is creating solid jobs, our governments generally have their fiscal houses in order, and Canada's population is forecast to continue growing at a decent pace. All of this bodes well for professional sports in Canada.

Lastly, let's not forget the increasing number of immigrants, who are slowly changing the landscape of Canada's demography. This will be great for soccer and could lead to the emergence of new professional sport leagues, such as one for cricket.

We had a blast writing this book and hope you had fun reading it. See you at the game!